"LIKE RIES AND TROUT'S OTHER BOOKS, *BOTTOM-UP MARKETING* IS BOTH WITTY AND ENGAGINGLY SKEPTICAL."   —*Inc.*

"Extensive advice on how to successfully implement a 'bottom-up' approach . . . filled with interesting case histories and anecdotes."   —*Creative: The Magazine of Promotion and Marketing*

"Packed with practical information to help you excel at marketing products, services or entire companies . . . provides a step-by-step procedure for developing a campaign."   —*Milwaukee Journal*

"Those delightful folks who gave you the word *positioning* are at it again . . . they were talking about marketing before most people knew there was such a thing."
                    —*Fort Worth Star Telegram*

"Entertaining and full of up-to-date marketing stories."
                    —*Marketing News*

"YOU'LL LEARN TO THINK DIFFERENTLY ABOUT MARKETING AND YOUR COMPETITORS AFTER READING THIS PUNCHY BOOK."
                    —*Planning Review*

Al Ries and Jack Trout are perhaps the country's foremost marketing strategists. Their New York City firm, Trout & Ries Inc., has developed marketing programs for many of America's leading corporations, including Burger King, Chase Manhattan, Citicorp, Digital Equipment, IBM, Merck, Paramount, Smith Kline & French and Weyerhaeuser. They are the best-selling authors of *Marketing Warfare*, also available in a Plume edition.

Bottom-Up Marketing

by
Al Ries

and
Jack Trout

A PLUME BOOK

PLUME

Published by the Penguin Group
Penguin Books USA Inc., 375 Hudson Street, New York, New York 10014, U.S.A.
Penguin Books Ltd, 27 Wrights Lane, London W8 5TZ, England
Penguin Books Australia Ltd, Ringwood, Victoria, Australia
Penguin Books Canada Ltd, 2801 John Street, Markham, Ontario, Canada L3R 1B4
Penguin Books (N.Z.) Ltd, 182-190 Wairau Road, Auckland 10, New Zealand

Penguin Books Ltd, Registered Offices: Harmondsworth, Middlesex, England

This is an authorized reprint of a hardcover edition
published by McGraw-Hill, Inc.

First Plume Printing, May, 1990
10 9 8 7 6 5

**Dedicated to the thousands of business people
who didn't read *Positioning*.**

**And the thousands of business people
who didn't read *Marketing Warfare*.**

May they see the light.

Contents

Chapter 9. Making the changes

You can't change the mind of the prospect. You have to make your strategy work by changing the product, the service, or the organization. You are bound to run into difficulties.

Chapter 10. Shifting the battlefield

When you're losing the battle, shift the battlefield. There are four types of battlefield shifts: shifting the audience, shifting the product, shifting the focus, and shifting the distribution.

Chapter 11. Shifting the battlefield at GM

Let's say you are Roger Smith at General Motors. How do you shift the battlefield to repel the European invaders at the high end of the market?

Chapter 12. Testing your strategy

How to test your strategy in advance with your prospects, your sales force, and the press.

Chapter 13. Selling your strategy

How to sell your strategy to top management in the event that you are not top management yourself.

Chapter 14. Getting the resources

How to get the necessary resources (spelled "money") to finance your marketing strategy

Chapter 15. Calling in the outsider

When should you call in an outsider to help you develop an effective marketing program? Should the outsider work on the tactic or the strategy?

Introduction

Our first two books were "textbooks" on the principles of communications and the principles of marketing.

The first book, *Positioning: The Battle for Your Mind,* was a textbook on communications. According to positioning theory, the human mind contains slots or positions which a company attempts to fill. This is easy to do if the position is empty, but difficult to do if the position is owned by a competitor. In the latter case a company must "reposition its competition" if it wants to get into the mind.

Our second book, *Marketing Warfare,* was a textbook on marketing. The new point of view brought to the marketing arena was the belief that marketing is not a single-sided process of serving the customer.

The true nature of marketing today is outwitting, outflanking, outfighting the competition. In short, marketing is war, where the enemy is your competitor and the ground to be won is the customer.

As with real war, there is no one way to fight a marketing war. Rather there are four: defensive, offensive, flanking, and guerrilla warfare. Knowing which type of warfare to fight is the first and most important decision you can make.

The third book

Unlike the first two, *Bottom-Up Marketing* is not a textbook. It is a self-help book designed for the business person who wants to get on the fast track.

In this competitive environment, according to a recent survey, more CEOs climb to the top of the corporate ladder through sales and marketing than any other function.

We live in an "age of competition." In almost every category, today's business arena has become warlike.

This change of environment has made the traditional "top-down" approach to marketing obsolete. What good are long-term strategic plans when you cannot predict future competitive moves?

How can you react to a competitor if your resources are tied up in a long-term plan?

Strategy and tactics

Bottom-Up Marketing does not ignore the principles of positioning or the principles of marketing warfare. Rather, the book integrates the two concepts. But it doesn't do so in the way you might expect.

Communications, as outlined in the *Positioning* book, are the tactics of a business. Typically they include a company's advertising, publicity, sales presentations, etc.

Marketing, as outlined in the *Marketing Warfare* book, is the strategy of a business. Typically the strategy of a company is spelled out in a document which is the end result of a strategic planning process.

A lot of strategic planning takes place today. Management has fallen in love with the concept. No self-respecting Fortune 500 company could live without a vice president of long-range strategic planning.

We are opposed to long-term strategic planning, mission statements, goals, business plans, annual budgets.

We believe that most managers today fail to understand the critical relationship between strategy and tactics. That's why they continue to be beguiled by the strategic planning process.

Traditional theory says that top management should first set the strategy for a marketing campaign. Then the strategy should be turned over to middle managers who select the tactics to use to execute the strategy.

We disagree. Our concept is just the opposite.

1

Tactics dictate strategies

After years of strategic work for some of America's largest companies, we have come to a revolutionary conclusion: Strategy should be developed from the bottom up, not from the top down. In other words, strategy should be developed from a deep knowledge and involvement in the actual tactics of the business itself.

Tactics should dictate strategies. That is, the communications tactic should dictate the marketing strategy.

Most marketing people believe the reverse. The accepted wisdom is that the grand strategy of the organization should be set first; then the tactics can follow.

Challenging the obvious

Some of the most productive lines of development in science, medicine, and business have been stimulated by challenging obvious truths. Riemann overthrew Euclid's fifth postulate, which states that through a given point there's not more than one parallel line to a given straight line. Physicists are still exploring the many consequences of Riemann geometry.

For every obvious truth there appears to be an opportunity for progress, be it in science or business.

"Strategy dictates tactics" is an axiom of business that may be so deeply ingrained in your mind that you cannot see that it's there. "I'm not sure who discovered America," said one first grader, "but I know it wasn't an Indian."

How deeply ingrained is the notion that strategy takes precedence over tactics?

First of all, nobody ever says "tactics and strategy." It's always the reverse. Furthermore, the reverse is so logical. First you decide what you want to do (the strategy) and then you decide how to do it (the tactics).

"Our plans miscarry because they have no aim," said Seneca. "When a man does not know what harbor he is making for, no wind is the right wind."

Who can argue with that?

We can. Christopher Columbus wanted to find a shortcut to India (the strategy) by sailing west instead of east (the tactic). He died thinking he was a failure because he never found the Indian continent he was looking for.

If he had let the tactic dictate the strategy, he might have realized that he had discovered America, a feat of far greater significance than finding a shortcut to India.

Columbus was a sailor, a very good sailor. He should have selected the tactic of sailing west precisely because everybody else was sailing east. (In marketing, we would call this approach a flanking move.)

Whatever was to be found by sailing west, Columbus would have found it first.

The sins of top-down thinking

Managers are obsessed with "what they want to do." What are long-term plans except a meticulous outline of where managers want their company to be in five years or ten years?

When you put the emphasis on strategy, or where you want to be in the years ahead, you commit one of the two cardinal sins of business: (1) the refusal to accept failure and (2) the reluctance to exploit success. Both sins result from top-down thinking.

Columbus refused to accept the fact that he hadn't found a route to India, and he didn't exploit the magnificent discovery he did make.

Companies that set the strategy first usually refuse to accept failure because they figure all that's needed to turn a project into a winner is a minor adjustment in tactics.

Back in the fifties, General Electric made the strategic decision to get into the mainframe computer business. After 14 years of effort and $400 million worth of losses, it finally threw in the towel. Those minor adjustments in tactics turned out to be a major waste of resources.

Suppose it had turned the process upside down. Instead of going east with IBM, Univac, Burroughs,

NCR, RCA, Control Data, Honeywell, and the other mainframe players, suppose it had gone west by itself.

GE had two choices. At the high end it could have introduced a supercomputer. At the low end it could have introduced a personal computer.

But at the time there was no market for either supercomputers or personal computers. Exactly. That's why either tactic would have allowed GE to be first in the mind for a new type of computer.

Whether either move would have been profitable is another matter. That would have depended on what the future had in store. (As it happened, both directions became enormously profitable for at least two companies. Cray at the high end. Apple at the low end.)

There was no guarantee that Columbus would find anything at the end of his voyage. But if anyone was going to find anything, it was going to be Columbus, because he was doing it first.

The same principle applies to marketing. The only sure tactic to use is to find a way to move into the mind first. And since you're first, there is no market for your product or service. You have to build the market by yourself.

A refusal to accept failure is often combined with a reluctance to exploit success. The only progress GE made in the mainframe business was in establishing the concept of "time-sharing." It accomplished this feat by being first to introduce the idea.

This success should have encouraged the company to put all its computer resources into a time-sharing line. But the concept didn't fit GE's strategy of becoming another IBM by marketing a full line of computers. So the opportunity was wasted.

In business you tend to see what you expect to see. Which is why top-down thinking is so dangerous. You tend to overlook any factors that aren't related to the success of your strategy.

Reversing the process

When you reverse the process, you can sometimes make important discoveries.

The research people at Vicks came up with a new liquid cold remedy which cleared up scratchy throats and running eyes, but unfortunately also put you to sleep. Which was a problem if you wanted to go to work or drive a car.

Instead of writing off the research, someone at Vicks came up with a brilliant idea. If the product puts you to sleep, let's position it as a nighttime cold remedy. In other words, "the first nighttime cold remedy" is an advertising tactic that will work because it's based on the proven principle of being first.

And it did. NyQuil went on to become the most successful new product in Vicks' history. NyQuil is now the No. 1 cold remedy.

The tactic (the first nighttime cold remedy) dictates the strategy (introduce a major new cold remedy product called "NyQuil").

What's a tactic?

A tactic is an idea. When you look for a tactic, you are looking for an idea.

But the notion of an idea is a nebulous one. What *kind* of idea? *Where* do you find one? These are the initial questions that must be answered.

In order to help you answer these questions, we propose using the following specific definition: A tactic is a *competitive mental angle.*

A tactic must have a *competitive* angle in order to have a chance of success. This does not necessarily mean a better product or service, but rather there must be an element of differentness. It could be smaller, bigger, lighter, heavier, cheaper, more expensive. It could be a different distribution system.

Furthermore, the tactic must be competitive in the total marketing arena, not just competitive in relation to one or two other products or services.

For example, Volkswagen's decision in the late fifties to introduce "the first" small car was an excellent competitive tactic. At the time General Motors was manufacturing nothing but big, heavily chromed patrol boats. The Beetle was a runaway success.

The VW Beetle was not the first small car on the market, of course. But it was the first car to occupy the "small" position in the mind. It made a virtue out of its size, while the others apologized for their small size by talking about "roominess."

"Think small," said the Volkswagen ads.

An example of a bad tactic was Seagram's idea in the sixties to introduce a new bourbon against the likes of Jim Beam and Old Grand-Dad. Benchmark bourbon has gone nowhere because it has no competitive angle.

Second, a tactic must have a competitive *mental* angle. In other words, the battle takes place in the mind of the prospect.

Competitors that do not exist in the mind can be ignored. There were plenty of pizza places with home delivery operations when Tom Monaghan launched Domino's. But nobody owned the home delivery position in the mind.

On the other hand, there are competitors who enjoy strong perceptions in the mind that do not agree with reality. It's the mental perception that must be considered in the selection of a tactic, not the reality.

A competitive mental *angle* is the point in the mind that allows your marketing program to work effectively. That's the point you must leverage to achieve results.

But a tactic is not enough. To complete the process, you need to turn the tactic into a strategy. (If the tactic is a nail, the strategy is a hammer.) You need both to establish a position in the mind.

What's a strategy?

A strategy is not a goal. Like life itself, a strategy ought to be focused on the journey, not the goal. Top-down thinkers are goal-oriented. They first determine what it is they want to achieve and then they try to devise ways and means to achieve their goals.

But most goals are simply not achievable. Goal-setting tends to be an exercise in frustration. Marketing, like politics, is the art of the possible.

When Roger Smith took over General Motors in 1981, he predicted that GM would eventually own 70 percent of the traditional Big Three domestic car market, up from about 66 percent in 1980.

To prepare for this awesome responsibility, GM began a $50 billion modernization program.

Currently, General Motors' share of the Big Three domestic market is 58 percent and falling. GM's North American auto operations are running several hundred million dollars a year in the red. His goal was simply not achievable because it was not based on a sound tactic.

In our definition, a strategy is not a goal. It's a *coherent marketing direction.*

A strategy is *coherent* in the sense that it is focused on the tactic that has been selected. Volkswagen had a big tactical success with the small car, but it failed to elevate this idea to a coherent strategy. It forgot about "small" and instead elected to bring into the U.S. market a family of big, fast, and expensive Volkswagens. But these tactics had already been preempted by other car manufacturers. This opened the way for the Japanese to take over the small car idea.

Second, a strategy encompasses coherent *marketing* activities. Product, pricing, distribution, advertising— all the activities that make up the marketing mix must be coherently focused on the tactic.

(Think of the tactic as a particular wavelength of light and the strategy as a laser tuned to that wavelength. You need both to penetrate the mind of the prospect.)

Finally, a strategy is a coherent marketing *direction.* Once the strategy is established, the direction shouldn't be changed.

The purpose of the strategy is to mobilize your resources to preempt the tactic. By commiting all your resources to one strategic direction you maximize the exploitation of the tactic without the limitation that the existence of a goal implies.

In marketing as in warfare, the safest strategy is rapid exploitation of the tactic. Rest is for losers. Winners keep the pressure on.

Tactic versus strategy

A tactic is a singular idea or angle. A strategy has many elements, all of which are focused on the tactic.

A tactic is an angle that is unique or different. A strategy may well be mundane.

A tactic is independent of time and relatively constant. A strategy unfolds over a period of time. A sale is a tactic used at one time or another by most of the retailers in America. A store that has a sale every day is a discount store, which is a strategy.

Some retailers have sharpened this tactic into a powerful strategy. Syms is a highly successful discount clothing store in 10 eastern and midwestern states. "At Syms," say the television commercials, "you'll never hear the word *sale*. An educated consumer is our best customer."

A tactic is a competitive advantage. A strategy is designed to maintain that competitive advantage.

A tactic is external to the product, service, or company. It may not even be a product the company makes. A strategy is internal. (Strategies often require a great deal of internal reorganization.)

A tactic is communications-oriented. A strategy is product-, service-, or company-oriented.

The principle of bottom-up marketing is simple: You work from the specific to the general, from the short term to the long term.

Note, too, the singular implication of bottom-up marketing. Find a tactic that will work and then build it into a strategy. Find one tactic, not two or three or four.

One strategy and a variety of tactics

Most managers think in terms of strategy and tactics. That is, they search for a strategy they can express in terms of many different tactics. The emphasis in traditional marketing is expanding sideways into different markets using a number of tactics.

The corporate strategy then gets more and more general to encompass a profusion of tactics.

When John M. Stafford became chief executive at Pillsbury, his first big move, according to *The Wall Street Journal,* was to establish a committee to write a lengthy explanation of the company's "Mission and Values." He probably believed in the Moses approach to management. First you go up the mountain to get the tablets. Then you come down from the mountain to put the Ten Commandments to work.

That approach didn't work for Stafford. Apparently the managers at Burger King and Pillsbury's other restaurant operations couldn't effectively execute the company's mission.

Especially the commandment that said "Thou shalt make a satisfactory profit margin." So Stafford was fired for breaking one of his commandments.

Most generals, be they military or marketing ones, do not like to focus on tactics. It takes the fun out of the process.

Most generals like to generalize. It's more in keeping with the prerogatives of higher office to work on the "mission and values" statement than it is to eat a Whopper at a Burger King. When you get to be a high priest of business, you feel the overwhelming urge to pontificate.

When you get to the top, you like to be "free." Free of all those messy tactical details of the business. Free to participate in the fun side of marketing, the development of the grand strategy.

Battles are won with tactics

Yet marketing battles are won or lost at the tactical level, not at the strategic level.

The Vietnam war was lost in Vietnam, not in Washington, D.C. In a marketing war, you have to start with the notion that it's the tactics that will determine your success or failure.

A tactic can be a rather small advantage. The tactic exploited by Tom Monaghan at Domino's was to focus on the home delivery of pizza only. In itself, not a tremendously exciting idea. But it was unique and different because no other chain was doing this.

Notice that Domino's tactic was one tactic, not a collection of tactics. The idea was built around home delivery only. Not home delivery plus take-out plus eat-in plus hamburgers plus hot dogs plus the works.

What made Domino's such a powerhouse were the strategic implications of the home delivery tactic. By building a nationwide chain of home-delivery-only units, Domino's was able to preempt the "home delivery of pizza in 30 minutes, guaranteed" concept.

Looking for tactics to fit the strategy

Traditional top-down thinkers sometimes think they are working from the bottom up when they're really not. They will spend hours sifting through possible tactics.

What they are usually doing, however, is looking for tactics that fit their predetermined strategy. "A home delivery chain doesn't fit our strategy" might have been the reaction of Pizza Hut. "We're in the restaurant business."

Result: Monaghan made a fortune and Pizza Hut missed an opportunity.

The flaw in thinking is clear. Managers will search the marketing arena looking for tactics. Since they have already decided what they want to do they are searching for ways to do it. Sounds logical, doesn't it?

An emphasis on change

The emphasis in bottom-up marketing is change in the organization. Without change in the product or service or price or distribution, any strategy is likely to be a meaningless string of words.

The emphasis in traditional top-down marketing is change in the environment. "In order to achieve our goal of a 10 percent increase in market share, we have to increase brand preference for our product," says the traditional thinker.

In other words, *you* don't change; you try to change the marketplace. This is top-down thinking at its very worst.

"The best strategic plan is useless," said Field Marshal Erwin Rommel, "if it cannot be executed tactically." Unfortunately, Rommel worked for one of history's most notorious top-down thinkers.

Remarks like this cost Rommel his life. Marketing is

a safer occupation than the military. Disagreeing with corporate strategy can only cost you your job.

The purpose of strategy

One of the most useless exercises in marketing is sitting around a conference table evaluating strategies.

There are no *good* strategies. There are strategies that work tactically and there are strategies that don't work tactically. If this is true, then what is the purpose of a strategy?

The purpose of the strategy is to keep the competition from adversely affecting your tactics.

One Domino's home delivery unit could easily have been neutralized by market leader Pizza Hut. With the strategy of expanding into a nationwide chain of home delivery units, Domino's effectively drove a powerful wedge into the competition.

The tactic is the angle that produces the results. The strategy is the organization of the company to produce the maximum tactical pressure.

In the Battle of France, the German tactic was to exploit the "seam" between the British Expeditionary Forces to the north and the French armies to the south. The strategy was to commit the bulk of the panzer divisions to an attack through the Ardennes.

The tactic dictates the strategy. Then the strategy drives the tactic. To say that one is more important than the other is to miss the essence of the bottom-up process. It's the relationship between the two that is the crucial aspect of marketing success.

What's more important in aircraft design: the engine or the wing?

Neither. It's the relationship between the two that determines whether or not your design will get off the runway.

The tactic is the idea that directly affects your business. Strategy gives wings to the tactic that can make your business soar.

Top down versus bottom up

Managers who plan from the top down are trying to force things to happen. Managers who plan from the bottom up are trying to find things to exploit.

Top-down managers chase existing markets. Bottom-up managers look for new opportunities.

Top-down managers are internally oriented. Bottom-up managers are externally oriented.

Top-down managers believe in long-term success and short-term losses. Bottom-up managers believe in short-term success and long-term success.

2

Going down
to the front

"Would these books have been born," Ian Fleming once asked himself, "if I had not been living in the gorgeous vacuum of a Jamaican holiday?"

"I doubt it," said the author of the James Bond novels.

If the warm Jamaican weather inspired Fleming, it was the cold Santa Cruz surf that did the job for Jack O'Neill.

A dedicated surfer, O'Neill got tired of freezing to death and invented the industry's first wetsuit. Today O'Neill Inc. is a multimillion-dollar wetsuit company.

Going down to the front, finding a competitive mental angle, then coming back to headquarters and making the changes necessary to exploit that angle is the essence of bottom-up marketing.

It's easier said than done.

Vice president in charge of the front?

If the tactic should dictate the strategy, then the crucial step in the entire marketing process is "going down to the front." Unfortunately, most companies don't have a vice president in charge of this function.

That spells opportunity for you, dear reader. Right off the bat, you have a golden opportunity to develop a brilliant marketing strategy for your company (or for yourself) because the field is so wide open.

Don't confuse going down to the front with "sending" someone down to the front. In most companies there's a lot of sending going on. There's personal sending, as in asking for reports from the sales force. There's also impersonal sending, as in commissioning a marketing research study.

There's nothing wrong with marketing research as long as you remember that marketing is a game of the future. Most marketing research is a report on the past.

Research tells you what prospects have already done, not necessarily what they are going to do. (They don't know what they're going to do, so don't confuse them by asking.)

There's nothing wrong with sending someone to the front either. But nothing is better than getting your information firsthand.

Too many managers think they can run a marketing operation from an office. "A desk," wrote novelist John LeCarre, "is a dangerous place from which to watch the world."

Bottom up, the Japanese way

Bottom-up marketing is not the same as the Japanese system of building a consensus from the bottom of the organization to the top. That's loading the responsibility for the success of the company on the back of the lowest-ranking individual in the corporate army.

"In the past, we didn't need strong commanders," says Jiro Tokuyama, the retired dean of the Nomura School of Advanced Management. In the high-growth era, Japanese companies prospered by making the same types of products as their competitors, only making them better and cheaper.

Or as Mr. Tokuyama puts it, "The whole trench itself moved."

Today one industry after another is finding that the old style of Japanese management (with incremental steps, consensus building, and decision making from the bottom up) doesn't move the corporate "trench" fast enough or in new directions.

Bottom-up marketing, Japanese-style, is more a question of who does the marketing, not of what is being done.

Sometimes you get lucky. Sometimes the raw recruit comes through. Sometimes the lower-ranking employee has the brilliant idea that turns the company into a big winner.

But timing is against the process. In the Japanese system, the concept has to work its way up the ladder. Consensus has to be reached on each rung. Odds are against the brilliant idea.

The best marketing moves rarely look like big winners in advance. More than likely the best marketing moves have already been considered and discarded by your competitors.

Marketing is a gin rummy game. You find some of your best ideas in the discard pile.

Any concept that would get unanimous approval in your own company is already being used by somebody else. That's one reason the Japanese system produces conformity in products as well as people.

What's the difference between a Hitachi, a JVC, a Panasonic, and a Toshiba videocassette recorder?

Not much. They are all beneficiaries (or victims) of the Japanese bottom-up style of consensus marketing. The differences have all been ironed out in the movement of the concept from the bottom to the top of the organization.

Bottom up, the authors' way

In our bottom-up system, marketing is not a question of "who." Marketing is a question of "what."

The first thing you need to decide is "what" tactic to use. That is, you need to select a tactic that will deliver a competitive mental angle. Then you have to decide how to build the tactic into a coherent marketing direction.

Only after these steps have been taken can you determine "who" should execute the strategy.

Most companies have their priorities reversed. They are organized around people with titles which imply what they should be doing.

Sales managers manage sales. Marketing managers manage marketing. Advertising managers manage advertising.

"Who does what to whom" is pretty clear in most organizations. What's missing is a sense of what needs to be done and a system for getting things done in the natural, logical order.

This book is not written for marketing managers, who don't usually have the authority to do the things we recommend. Nor is it written for top managers, who may have the authority but often lack the perceptual skills to see things as they really are.

This book is written for anyone who wants to practice the principles of bottom-up marketing without the restrictions imposed by an organization chart.

If you're not at the top of the ladder, you may have to expend a certain amount of energy to get the fruits of your labor eaten by your superiors. Spend the time—that's an essential part of the process.

Information, not confirmation

Before going down to the front, you should ask yourself one question: Am I looking for information or confirmation?

Too many marketing people never do go down to the front. They go through the motions, looking for facts that will confirm their previously formed opinion of what should be done.

To a certain extent we are all victims of our own rhetoric. We preach the philosophy that managers ought to be decisive. So we're decisive, even before we have enough information as a basis on which to decide.

Leave your decisiveness back in the office when you go down to the front. Bring only a keen eye for observation and an open mind. The keen eye is optional; the open mind is not.

Where you need to be decisive is in going down to the front in the first place. Many managers put off

"seeing for themselves" because they have more important things to do.

Nothing is more important than visiting the scene of
the action. If you put it off until you have the time, you
will find that it's too late. You have already made up
your mind based on the second-hand information that
leaks into it. You will find yourself going down to the
front for confirmation, not for information. Better not
to go at all.

Observe, don't judge

When you get there, your problems have just begun.

Observing is not an easy process. The human mind is
quick to judge. Most of the time, quick-wittedness is an
advantage. But not when you are going down to the
front.

You must let yourself see things without instantly
judging them. Respect the facts, even though they
might be contrary to your expectations.

One way to overcome the mind's tendency to see
things in its own image is to write the facts down on a
piece of paper. Then read your notes later. An idea
your mind may have rejected as irrelevant may suddenly become the most relevant idea in the world.

Where is the front?

The front line of a marketing war is not where you
might expect to find it.

It's not the supermarket, the drugstore, or the customer's office. The front line is the mind of the prospect.

Going down to the front means putting yourself in a position to explore what customers and prospects might be thinking. (To become a good fisherman, you have to think like a fish.)

In the motion picture *Big,* Tom Hanks has the body of a man but the mind of a 13-year-old kid. Naturally, a toy company CEO instantly makes Tom a vice president.

The front can be in your own home, watching a spouse in the process of deciding which brand to buy or not to buy.

Ask why. Ask why he or she decided to buy a particular brand of toothpaste or shampoo. And don't confine your questions to just your own product category. A good marketing person is one who has a feel for a variety of marketing battles, not just his or her own.

If you don't explore a variety of marketing battles, you tend to get the feeling that everybody in the world spends his or her time evaluating the brands in your product category.

First impressions count

Don't be suspicious of your first impressions. Prospects act on their first impressions.

Don't fight the feeling of looking foolish. In some ways the most naive-sounding questions can turn out to be the most profound.

The worst mistake of all is to bring too much baggage to the front. When you are loaded down with the facts of your own product or service or company, you can't possibly put yourself in the prospect's shoes.

Ideally one wants to go to the front knowing almost nothing about the product or service. That way you can objectively evaluate the situation.

It's hard to do. The emphasis in Corporate America is not on the visit to the front. It's on the "briefing" that takes place ahead of time. The briefer's job is to convince you that he or she already knows all there can possibly be known about the situation.

You, the briefee, have to take everything with a grain of salt until you can see for yourself.

What are you looking for?

You are looking for an angle. A fact, an idea, a concept, an opinion on the part of the prospect that conflicts with the positions held by your competitors.

Take laundry detergents, for example. What does detergent advertising suggest that customers are looking for?

Cleanliness. That's why Tide gets clothes "white." Cheer gets clothes "whiter than white." And Bold goes all the way to "bright."

Did you ever watch a person take clothes out of a dryer? If you read the ads, you might think he or she puts on sunglasses so the glare won't ruin the eyes.

Most people hardly look at the clothes at all. But they almost always smell them to see if they smell "fresh."

This observation led Unilever to introduce Surf, a detergent whose sole distinguishing characteristic is that it contains twice as much perfume as the competition. Result: Surf came in and grabbed 12 percent of the $3.5 billion U.S. detergent market.

Did you ever watch a commuter buy a cup of coffee to carry on a train or bus? He or she will often carefully rip off a drinking hole in the lid so the coffee won't spill during the trip.

Someone at the Handi-Kup Division of Dixie Products noticed. Handi-Kup introduced a plastic lid with the drinking hole built in.

Some angles are hard to spot because customers express them in the negative. The Adolph Coors Company invented light beer. (Even today there are fewer calories in regular Coors than in Michelob Light.) Yet Coors ignored its own invention until Miller introduced Lite beer.

It was hard to ignore. Before Lite saw the light of day, any Denver bartender could have told you how their customers ordered a Coors.

"Give me a Colorado Kool-Aid."

Coors could have preempted the light category with a major advertising program. It didn't.

Miller did. So today Miller Lite outsells Coors and Coors Light combined.

Most angles are hard to spot because they almost never look like big winners in advance. (If they did, others would already be using them.) Marketing bombshells burst very quietly.

"Great ideas," said Albert Camus, "come into the world as gently as doves. Perhaps, then, if we listen attentively, we shall hear amid the uproar of empires and nations a faint flutter of wings, the gentle stirring of life and hope."

When you saw your first bottle of Lite beer, did you say, "This brand is going to become, behind Budweiser, the biggest-selling beer in America"?

Or did you say, "Here's another Gablinger's"?

When you saw your first Toys "Я" Us store, did you say, "This is going to be a $3 billion business selling one-fourth of all the toys in America"?

Or did you say to yourself, "Why did they letter the R backwards?"

Did you buy a McDonald's franchise in 1955 when it would have cost you all of $950?

Or did you wait in line saying to yourself, "How can they make money selling hamburgers for 15 cents?"

Did you buy Xerox stock in 1958? Andy Warhol soup cans in 1968? A BMW in 1973? A condo in Manhattan in 1979?

Did you buy Japanese yen in 1987? Or in 1986? Or in any previous year?

Did you save your baseball cards? Your Superman comic books?

Opportunities are hard to spot because they don't look like opportunities. They look like angles. A lighter beer, a more expensive car, a cheaper hamburger, a store that sells only toys.

You have to take that angle or tactic and build it into a strategy before you can unleash its power.

Chief executives tend to lose touch

The bigger the company, the more likely it is that the chief executive has lost touch with the front lines. This might be the single most important factor limiting the growth of a corporation.

All other factors favor size. Marketing is war and the first principle of warfare is the principle of force. The larger army, the larger company, has the advantage.

But the larger company gives up some of that advantage if it cannot keep itself focused on the marketing battle that takes place in the mind of the customer.

The shootout at General Motors between Roger Smith and Ross Perot illustrates the point. When he was on the GM board, Ross Perot spent his weekends buying cars. He was critical of Roger Smith for not doing the same.

"We've got to nuke the GM system," Perot said. He advocated atom-bombing the heated garages, chauffeur-driven limousines, executive dining rooms.

Chauffeur-driven limousines for a company trying to sell cars? Top management's disconnection with the marketplace is the biggest problem facing big business.

If you're a busy CEO, how do you gather objective information on what is really happening? How do you get around the propensity of middle management to tell you what they think you want to hear?

How do you get the bad news as well as the good?

One possibility is "going in disguise" or unannounced. This would be especially useful at the distributor or retailer level. In many ways this is analogous to the king who dresses up as a commoner and mingles with his subjects. Reason: To get honest opinions of what's happening.

Like kings, chief executives rarely get honest opinions from their ministers. There's just too much intrigue going on at the court.

The sales force, if you have one, is a critical element in the equation. The trick is how to get a good honest evaluation of competition out of them. The best thing you can do is to praise honest information. Once the word gets around that a CEO prizes honesty and reality, a lot of good information might be forthcoming.

Another aspect of the problem is the allocation of your time. Quite often it is taken up with too many activities that keep you from visiting the front. Too many boards, too many committees, too many testimonial dinners. According to one survey, the average CEO spends 30 percent of his or her time on "outside activities." He or she spends 17 hours a week attending meetings and 6 hours a week preparing for meetings.

Since the typical top executive works 61 hours a week, that leaves only 20 hours for everything else, including managing the operation and going down to the front.

No wonder chief executives delegate the marketing function. That's a mistake.

Marketing is too important to be turned over to an underling. If you delegate anything, you should delegate the chairmanship of the next fund-raising drive. (As you've perhaps noticed, the Vice President of the United States attends the state funerals, not the President.)

Next thing to cut back on are the meetings. Instead of talking things over, go out and see for yourself. As General Secretary Gorbachev told President Reagan, on the occasion of the President's first trip to the Soviet Union, "It is better to see once than to hear a hundred times."

"The devil is in the details"

How should a CEO operate? Andrews Grove of Intel said it best. "There's a tendency at the senior and middle-manager level to be too big-picturish and too superficial. There is a phrase, 'The devil is in the details.' One can formulate brilliant global strategies whose executability is zero. It's only through familiarity with details—the capability of the individuals who have to execute, the marketplace, the timing—that a good strategy emerges."

Grove sums up his approach in one sentence: "I like to work up from details to big pictures."

Amen. This is the essence of *Bottom-Up Marketing*.

As you may have noticed, Intel has been on a roll while General Motors has been going downhill rapidly.

The devil is in the details. That's also where you'll find the tactic to turn into the brilliant strategy.

It was in a seedy roadside motel near Washington, D.C., that Kemmons Wilson got the concept for Holiday Inns. The place not only charged $6 for Wilson and his wife, but $2 for each of their five children as well. Highway robbery, he thought.

Wilson returned to Memphis determined to build a family motel where children would stay free. The next year he opened the first Holiday Inn.

You don't have to take a trip to find an angle. Jim Dyer invented the highly successful *Pocket Organizer* based on his own personal way of organizing his notes.

Richard James accidentally dropped a tension spring on the floor and it "walked." Forty-three years later, the Slinky is still a favorite toy for children and adults.

Mary Phelps Jacobs was only 19 years old when she had her maid make an undergarment from two lace handkerchiefs and a pink ribbon. She called her invention a brassiere, patented it, and later sold her patent for $15,000 to the Warners Brothers Corset Company.

Small companies have an advantage

Sophia Collier was 21 years old when she launched Soho Natural Soda back in 1977. Today her company is well on its way to topping $100 million in sales.

A vegetarian who once lived on a Hopi Indian reservation, Ms. Collier obviously got the concept for Soho out of her own lifestyle. At first, the distributors she had to deal with didn't believe there was a market. "Natural soda," they'd say, "isn't that a contradiction in terms?"

And so it is. But that's the competitive mental angle that Sophia Collier and her partner Connie Best brilliantly exploited.

Reese Jones was operating a Macintosh users' group out of his own home when the group wanted to share a computer printer located in another part of the house. Rather than going to the expense of stringing wire, Jones used the alternate circuit on the telephone lines, inventing a connector in the process.

Today his company (Farallon) sells more than a million dollars' worth of PhoneNet connectors a month.

Small companies are mentally closer to the front than big companies. That might be one reason they are growing more rapidly.

A key measure of growth is employment. In the past six years, employment declined 9 percent at companies with 1000 or more workers. In the same period, employment increased 17 percent at companies with fewer than 100 workers.

Big companies have problems getting down to the front. The Charge of the Light Brigade was ordered by an officer who wasn't there looking at the territory.

T. K. Quinn, former chairman of General Electric Credit, once said, "Not a single distinctively new electric home appliance has ever been created by one of the giant concerns—not the first washing machine, electric range, dryer, iron or ironer, electric lamp, refrigerator, radio, toaster, fan, heating pad, razor, lawn mower, freezer, air conditioner, vacuum cleaner, dishwasher, or grill."

It wasn't Xerox that invented xerography. It was Chester Carlson. It wasn't IBM that built the first computer. It was John Mauchly and J. Presper Eckert.

The problems of the CEO

If you're the chief executive officer, you have one big advantage in the development of strategy: you can approve the program and it runs.

Unfortunately, the CEO is often the person most out of touch with the marketplace. (You don't get to be CEO by pleasing the customer. You get to be CEO by pleasing the previous CEO, who is usually even more out of touch than you are.)

One problem is the number of management layers between the top and the bottom. The more layers, the more you are insulated from the market. The rich white frosting at the top of many corporations is increasingly divorced from the soggy realities at the bottom of the cake.

The layers tend to filter out the bad news and pass along only the good news. When things start to go bad, the CEO is often the last to know.

Reducing the number of layers is one way for a chief executive to get psychologically closer to the front. One study of 60 companies showed that the top performers had less than four management layers; poor ones had about eight.

Regardless of the number of layers in the organization, it's the organization itself that makes it difficult for a chief executive to go down to the front.

Most visits to the battleground are turned by lower-level people into a ceremonial "Grand Tour." Everything is cleaned up and carefully orchestrated to look good.

You are encouraged to consider your visit as a morale-building trip, not as an information-gathering venture. "Blow a little sunshine into the trenches," says the tour guide.

Then there's the corporate entourage. Some CEOs feel they can't travel without a driver, bodyguard, valet, assistant, secretary, speech writer, advance man, chef, hair dresser, etc. An idea has a hard time breaking through this protective phalanx.

Some CEOs make a special effort to get to the bottom of things. "When we started in biotechnology," said Monsanto's Richard J. Mahoney, "I found I was approving stuff I didn't understand, so I took a series of tutorials, went into the lab, put on a coat, and did the tests myself."

Harvard political scientist Richard E. Neustadt noted that a successful business executive must actively seek information the way a political leader should.

"It is not information of a general sort that helps a President see personal stakes," wrote Neustadt. "It is the odds and ends of tangible detail that, pieced together in his mind, illuminate the underside of issues put before him. To help himself he must reach out as widely as he can for every scrap of fact, opinion, gossip, bearing on his own interests and relationships as President."

The problems of the CEG

At the bottom of the corporate cake sits the chief executive gofer.

If you are the newest, the youngest, the least experienced member of the team, you have an enormous advantage. You are at the front, oftentimes saturated by the very details that CEOs would give their eyeteeth to know.

What an opportunity! Yet so many young people throw that opportunity away by looking in rather than out. They focus their attention on what's happening inside the company rather than on what's happening on the outside among customers and prospects. They tell their managers what they want to hear rather than what they ought to know.

There's a certain logic in all of this. You don't get promoted by telling your boss that he or she is wrong. You get promoted by laying on the positives to your superior. ("He's a smart kid. He thinks just like me.")

If you, dear reader, are in your first job, you ought to learn how to tell it like it is. Not, we hasten to add, to express your opinions, but rather to report the realities of the battles taking place in the market. Only by learning how to be an accurate observer of the tactical war can you develop the marketing skills that will lead to strategic brilliance later.

Too many beginners want to begin at the top. That's why so many freshly minted MBAs wind up working for consulting firms.

Companies are starting to get wise, however. "When I meet a young consultant without any field experience," said Frank Perdue, "I really can't believe it. People need to understand that they don't know everything about everything, and that it's no sin to start at the bottom and work up."

Or as Harry Truman once said: "The only things worth learning are the things you learn after you know it all."

The problems in the middle

The action in most corporations is in the middle. Top management sets the strategy, but it's the middle managers who must translate their companies' strategies into tactics.

People in the middle are often out of touch with the marketplace. There's no time to go down to the front. There are too many meetings to attend, too many planning documents to write, too much paperwork to take care of. (If families were run the way business runs, the kids wouldn't get their allowances until they filled out their expense accounts for the week before.)

The planning process in most companies contributes to the isolation of middle managers. Many managers don't have the time to visit the front. They're too busy writing the planning document supposedly based on their trips to the battlefields.

When they do bump into reality, often by accident, they are sometimes horrified to find that their plans are based on myths rather than facts.

Take the boom in financial services companies. Everybody is selling, promoting, and marketing financial services.

Stockbrokers don't sell stocks anymore. They sell financial services: annuities, mutual funds, municipal bonds.

Life insurance companies don't just sell you life and property insurance anymore. To quote from a Travelers ad, they sell "diversified financial services" including mortgage financing, retirement programs, mutual funds, HMOs, and PPOs.

Commercial banks want to be your financial partner for life, with credit cards, insurance, you name it. (Open an account with Citibank or Chase and your mailbox will be full every day. You'll find offers for financial services you wouldn't believe even existed.)

Go down to the front lines of the financial services war and listen to customers and prospects. Did you ever hear a customer use the words "financial services"?

As in "Let's go down to the Savings & Loan, dear, and get some financial services."

Customers don't generalize; they *specificize*. They talk in terms of mortgages, stocks, car insurance, annuities, home equity loans.

Yet companies trying to sell these customers are doing just the opposite. They promote themselves as suppliers of a full range of financial services. In the military analogy we call this "attacking on a wide front." And it almost never works.

The problems of the entrepreneur

In a word, money. In every other way a handful of entrepreneurs-to-be have a big advantage over millions of corporate managers.

Entrepreneurs are down at the front. Their ideas and concepts tend to spring from their own personal experiences. They have the power to make decisions since they don't have to seek the approval of others. As a result a vast majority of the big marketing successes have sprung from the entrepreneurial ranks.

Money, however, is a major barrier to success. What stops many entrepreneurs is not the lack of ideas but the lack of venture capital. In many fields today the price of admission starts at a million and goes up from there.

Federal Express soaked up more than $80 million in outside money before it started to make a profit. And Fred Smith threw in several million of his own to feed the engines.

No easy way

Whether you are an individual entrepreneur or a corporate manager, whether you work for a big company or a small one, whether you're at the top or the bottom of the organization or somewhere in between, there's no easy way to practice bottom-up marketing.

There is, however, an enormous opportunity if you are willing to make the struggle. So few are doing it.

Most managers are up there looking down, armed with their corporate mission statements and five-year plans.

They are easy marks for bottom-up thinkers.

3

Monitoring the trends

How things have changed in 30 years.

One of the most persistent myths in marketing is the notion of change. How have things changed in the last three decades?

Let's look at those dramatic changes from the point of view of an average day for one of the authors.

A day in the life

This morning the alarm rang and I got out of bed. I showered, shaved, got dressed, ate breakfast, and drove to the train station.

I did exactly the same thing 30 years ago.

Maybe if we look a little closer, we'll see the dramatic differences. Maybe it was the soap I showered with? Nope, it was Ivory both times.

Big change in shampoo, though. I used to use Prell. I now use something called Style shampoo. (My daughter, however, uses Prell.)

Let's move from the shower to the lavatory. What a difference. My Atra has two blades instead of the single-blade Gillette razor I used to use. My deodorant is now an antiperspirant. My toothpaste is Crest instead of Colgate. (In the early sixties the ADA seal of approval got me to switch.)

When I get dressed, however, I really begin to notice the dramatic differences. For some reason, I'm not wearing a T-shirt anymore. (Perhaps it's a trend toward simplicity.)

There are no laces in my shoes, no cuffs on my pants, and I don't wear a tiepin. To counterbalance the trend toward simplicity, I put a handkerchief in my pocket and a collarpin on my shirt. My watch is powered by a battery instead of by swinging my arm. My wallet goes into my jacket instead of my pants pocket.

I had orange juice and cereal for breakfast, just like I did 30 years ago. I also had coffee, but without the cream, without the sugar, and without the caffeine.

Then I drive to the station in a car with an internal combustion engine. But today it has eight cylinders instead of six and uses unleaded gasoline.

At the office, I still have meetings like I used to, write letters out in longhand like I used to. I have a secretary who types the letters on a machine that still looks like a typewriter although it's actually a computer.

My telephone, however, is a lot different. It used to be black; it's now white.

After work I come home and do what I did 30 years ago: watch television and think about how much my life has changed.

If I had to name the two most important and dramatic changes in 30 years of living, they would have to be the two blades in my razor and the unleaded gasoline in my automobile.

I can't wait for the unbelievable changes that are going to take place in the decades to come. Three blades in my razor? Alcohol instead of gasoline in my tank?

The hype versus the reality

If you read your daily newspaper or national magazine, you get an entirely different picture of reality. There are incredible, earth-shaking changes taking place every day.

"The eighties are over. Greed goes out of style," said the cover story of a recent issue of *Newsweek*.

Greed goes out of style? Just like that? You better believe it because *Newsweek* said it did: "Decades are not a function of calendar time. They are trends, values and associations, bundled up and tied together in the national memory. They begin and end in the middle of the night sometime when everyone is looking the other way."

Did Charles Lazarus, who made $60 million as chief executive of Toys "Я" Us in 1987, take a Peace Corps job in South America in 1988? We doubt it.

"Hey, brother, peace be with you." Is that the way they now greet each other on Wall Street? Did anything really change in America as *Newsweek* said it did?

When you begin to monitor the trends, keep in mind that most of the trends are manufactured to sell newspapers or magazines, not to help you market your products.

Yet marketing people tend to believe the hype rather than the reality. "The consumer marketing equation continues to change in profound and irreversible ways," said one management guru. "So a basic change in attitude is needed: from managing businesses to managing change."

Where are all those changes? What happened to the paperless, cashless, checkless society?

What happened to the Third Wave, Megatrend, Second Industrial Revolution, Information-Oriented Society where everyone works at home in front of a computer/picturephone terminal?

As a matter of fact, what happened to the picturephone?

Did you get your helicopter yet? Where is the marvelous device that was going to replace your car and make the superhighway obsolete?

Have you been getting your electronic newspaper delivered daily through your television set as promised two decades ago?

The reality never seems to catch up with the hype. The future always seems to be just over the next hill.

Yet what happens when you sit down to write a marketing plan? "Everything is rapidly changing in our industry" tends to be your first thought.

Like the waves on the ocean, everything is constantly changing. But these are short-term changes that block your ability to see long-term trends.

If you are in the food business, for example, all the hype is focused on chicken and fish. "Beef is dead. Everybody is eating chicken and fish."

In reality, the per-capita consumption of beef exceeds that of chicken and fish combined.

But beef consumption is declining, you might think. In reality, the per-capita consumption of beef has increased in each of the last three years. That's just a wave, however, on the ocean of change. What might happen in the future is another matter.

The office of the future

In recent years, no myth has received as much hype. Yet the office of today looks a lot more like the office of the past than it does the "office of the future."

This morning you probably got a cup of coffee, read your mail, dictated a few letters, made a few phone calls, and extracted a few pieces of paper from your file drawers. Your counterpart in Corporate America probably did the same thing ... 50 years ago.

Whatever happened to the office of the future?

It's ironic that the most dramatic change in office operations today has nothing to do with electronics. It's the arrival of Federal Express, the Pony Express of the twentieth century.

Whatever happened to the computer-driven office automation system?

Like so many other overhyped ideas, the "office of the future" continues to lurk somewhere out there in the future and never seems to get any closer to reality.

Myths tend to feed on themselves. That's why going down to the front doesn't mean reading your favorite newspaper or business publication.

Once an idea like the office of the future gets written about, it continues to get press. Hype creates hype.

What do you think editors and reporters read? That's right, the output of other editors and reporters. It's a great deal easier than generating original material.

You can't predict the future

So don't plan on it.

No sooner had *Megatrends* hit the bookstores predicting a surge in the Sunbelt when just the opposite occurred. The northeast took off, against the trend, against the predictions of the "experts."

The October 26, 1987 issue of *Fortune* arrived on the newsstands October 12 with a cover picture of Alan Greenspan, America's No. 1 economist and the Federal Reserve chairman.

"Why Greenspan is bullish," said the *Fortune* cover. One week later the Dow-Jones industrial average dropped 508 points, losing 22.6 percent of its value. Greenspan missed Black Monday by a mile.

Way back in 1917, the Interior Department predicted that America had only 27 years of oil left. Fifty-one years later, in 1975, the U.S. government prediction stood at 12 years. Did we run out of oil in 1987?

One problem is that short-term trends are self-correcting, just like the stock market. An increase in beef consumption results in an increase in beef prices which results in a decrease in beef consumption.

Likewise, the demand for network television advertising time has softened. It wouldn't take much reduction in network TV pricing to reinflate the demand.

A fatal flaw

The fatal flaw in many marketing plans is a strategy based on "predicting the future."

Seldom are the predictions obvious. Usually, they are so buried in the assumptions that you need a degree in rhetoric to ferret them out.

The most common flaw is extrapolating a trend. If you believed the prognosticators of a few years ago, everyone today is eating broiled fish or mesquite-barbecued chicken.

The key point is that basic habits change very slowly and the press often magnifies small changes. The result is that companies misread the situation. This is why McDonald's and Burger King jumped on the chicken bandwagon. It's why Avon is moving away from their "shop at home" concept.

Equally as bad as extrapolating a trend is the common practice of assuming the future will be a replay of the past. When you assume that nothing will change, you are predicting the future just as surely as when you assume that something will change.

Remember Peter's Law: "The unexpected always happens."

The story of Slice

Slice is a carbonated soft drink that was introduced by Pepsi-Cola as both a sugared product and a diet product.

We would have recommended that Slice be a diet product only. (Because of its fruit juice sweeteners, Diet Slice has 28 calories.)

The reason for this recommendation is to better position Slice as a fitness and health product. In other words, a diet-only Slice would have narrowed the "focus" of the product, always a good strategy in a marketing war.

A diet-only strategy also would have ignored the sugar element, which represents 80 percent of the market. So Slice was introduced as a two-way player. It's done well but, in our opinion, not as well as it could have done as a pure diet product.

As things turned out, the diet segment of the soft drink market is growing at the expense of the sugared versions. Currently 27 percent of all Cokes sold, for example, are of the diet variety.

With Slice, as you might expect, the diet variety outsells the sugar version. By focusing on the diet version only, we believe that the product would have an even higher market share. The advertising could have been better focused on fitness and health. "Slice adds the fruit juices and subtracts the calories," for example.

Individual products don't always "follow the market." In spite of the fact that sugared products represent 73 percent of the cola market, the diet version of Caffeine-Free Coke outsells the sugared version more than four to one.

You can't predict the enemy

Generals who make military plans based on "knowing" what the enemy is going to do are "predicting the enemy," which is another way of predicting the future. They usually turn out to be losing generals.

Winning generals tend to make military plans that are workable regardless of what the enemy does. This is the essence of good strategy.

When you predict what the enemy is going to do, you are buying a lottery ticket with your company's future at stake.

Gambling may be all right in Las Vegas, in Atlantic City, or on Wall Street. But it's not good enough for marketing.

You can create the future

There's also a difference between "predicting" the future and "creating" the future.

When you predict the future, you are counting on a change in consumer behavior that will be taking place sometime in the near future. You're standing there with your surfboard, waiting.

When you create the future, you introduce a product or service whose very success "creates" a trend. In essence, you are untapping a latent interest in a new category of product. In the military analogy, we call this a flanking move.

All good flanking moves create their own future. They don't depend on developments outside of their immediate area.

Orville Redenbacher's Gourmet Popping Corn took a chance that people would pay twice as much for a high-end popcorn. Not a bad risk in today's affluent society.

Stouffer's took a chance that people would pay $3 for a TV dinner. It gave the product a $3 concept (low-calorie gourmet food) and a $3 name (Lean Cuisine).

Stouffer's created the gourmet frozen entree category. It sells more than $300 million worth of Lean Cuisine a year.

Trends versus fads

There are some long-term trends that are very different from the short-term changes constantly taking place.

Cigarette smoking declined from 37 percent of the adult population in 1970 to 33 percent in 1980. (That 4 percent decline sent shock waves through the tobacco industry.)

Long-term trends happen very slowly. People don't wake up in the middle of the night and stop smoking.

In 25 years adult consumption of coffee has fallen from 3.1 cups a day to 1.7 cups a day.

Will the decline continue? You can be reasonably sure it will. Among adults 60 years of age and older, 79 percent drink coffee. Among adults in the 20-to-29 age bracket, only 41 percent drink coffee. Coffee consumption will continue to decline.

How can you tell the difference between a fad and a trend? Between a picturephone and a videocassette recorder? Between a wave and a tide?

It's not easy. For one thing, a trend usually has to be observed for a decade or more. Even then, you can't always be sure.

Beef consumption, for example, declined from 88 pounds per capita in 1975 to 77 pounds in 1980. Then beef consumption started to increase.

Just when everyone thought that jogging was going to replace night baseball as America's favorite sport, jogging experienced a sharp decline. So what can one predict for the current Nautilus craze?

It's hard to tell.

Nobody smokes anymore

Another way to tell the difference between a trend and a fad is to look for a cause and effect. The decline of cigarette smoking is not just a decline; it's also the effect of the Surgeon General's report on smoking in 1964 and the antismoking publicity that report generated.

More than half of all male adults smoked in 1964. Today less than 40 percent do. (For women, the percentage who smoke fell from 33 to 29 percent.)

An even more significant fact is that two-thirds of all physicians who smoked in 1964 have quit. Because of their influence on the rest of the population, these nonsmoking physicians will likely cause the trend to continue.

Even the strongest of trends tend to get exaggerated. (Two women are having lunch and one says to the other, "Nobody smokes anymore.")

She's only partially right. In 25 years, the net decline in the percentage of adult women who smoke was 4 percent.

In action and excitement, watching women stop smoking ranks right up there with watching the grass grow.

"Nobody smokes anymore" is in the same category as "nobody eats white bread anymore." (Seventy percent of all bread sold today is still white.)

Yet smoking cigarettes and eating white bread are clearly on the decline. It's a strong trend. Which brings up another difference between a fad and a trend.

Trends involve slow change

"Everybody works" is another one of those trends that get exaggerated. Today, among women with children under 6 years old, about 55 percent have a job.

But 8 years ago, about 45 percent of women in that same category also worked. So that booming trend (and it is a definite trend) represents about a 1 percent increase in employment per year.

"People are getting older." Yes, they're living longer, so the median age of the population is moving up. Before you revise your marketing plan, however, you might take a look at the reality instead of the hype.

Back in 1950, the median age was 30 years. Today it's around 32. It's taken almost 40 years for the population to age 2 years.

Even these numbers hide one of the periodic waves that sweep through the statistics. From 1950 to 1970, the median age declined from 30 to 28 years.

So we have had two decades of "people are getting younger" hype followed by two decades of "people are getting older" hype.

There have been a lot more changes in the hype than in the population.

A trend usually involves slow change. A fad is like fashion: it usually starts much faster and ends more abruptly.

The stock market crash of 1987 illustrates the difference. If you had bought stock on the last trading day of 1986 and sold it on the last trading day of 1987, how badly would you have been hurt?

In other words, how bad a year was 1987? Actually

the Dow-Jones Industrial Average finished 1986 at 1896 and closed a year later at 1939, so your stocks, on average, should have been 2.3 percent ahead for the year.

The stock market crash was a fad in the midst of a long-term trend of rising stock prices.

You knew the digital watch was going to be a fad when sales took off overnight. You should have known that wine coolers were going to cool off when sales exploded two years in a row.

On the other hand, sales of microwave ovens took off very slowly. Today more than half of all households have a microwave oven, a higher percentage than have dishwashers.

In the office environment, the comparable product is the facsimile machine. Like the microwave oven, facsimile also started very slowly.

Today fax is building up a head of steam that in the long run will be hard for the U.S. Postal Service, facsimiles' natural competitor, to stop.

Another difference between a fad and a trend is the fact that the fad gets all the press. A fad is newsworthy because it represents something that's happening rapidly. Trends get much less press because they take place slowly.

You can take a bath by jumping on a trend too quickly. Sure, air travel in the United States has increased in the wake of deregulation. So Braniff's CEO Harding Lawrence bought 40 new planes and opened 16 new routes in one day. The move turned 1978's $45 million net income into a $44 million loss in 1979 as the economy slid into a recession and fuel costs doubled.

A rising level of expectations

There is a trend, however, that accounts for much of the success of high-end products like Rolex watches and Jaguar cars. This trend might be called a rising level of expectations.

Compare the quarter century between 1960 and 1985, for example. The median family income in 1960 was $5620. Twenty-five years later, it was $27,735, almost five times as much.

Maybe the 27 grand wouldn't buy five times as many goods and services, but most people felt better off because they had more money in their pockets. (Actually they were better off. The consumer price index in 1985 was only 3.6 times the 1960 average.)

Not only do consumers have more dollars in their pockets, they have more degrees on their walls.

In 1960 fewer than 8 percent of adults 25 years and older had a college degree. By 1985 almost 20 percent did. Would a Harvard graduate settle for a Chevrolet? Or a Princeton alumnus drive a Plymouth? Bring on the Volvo and the BMW, whether they can afford them or not.

The role of research

You might think in a "monitoring the trends" discussion that we'd be making a big deal about research.

We're not.

Most of the numbers you need to develop an effective marketing plan can be obtained from your local library, the U.S. government, or your favorite trade publication. This is research that tells you what people have actually done.

When you use research to try to find out what people will do, you run into problems.

People often respond to questions in a way they deem is the most socially acceptable. This is especially true in focus groups where other people are looking on behind the one-way mirrors.

The trick is to find a way to get the answers that people keep in the closet. Who wants to admit they eat fast food instead of nutritious food? How many business executives will admit they hate to write letters or they find personal computers intimidating? Who will admit to overusing the telephone?

The role of reversal

There's always a market for an opposite point of view.

In the last 100 years, the most one-sided presidential election in American history was in 1920. In that election, Republican Warren G. Harding got 61.6 percent of the votes compared with Democrat James M. Cox, who got 34.9 percent. (Socialist Eugene V. Debs received the other 3.5 percent.)

In the biggest presidential election loss in the twentieth century, the loser still managed to get more than a third of the vote. In many product categories today, the leading brand doesn't have that much of the market.

What creates a Democrat? Many of them are created by Republicans. When labor leaders see which party gets the most support from business leaders, guess which party gets the labor vote.

What creates a Republican? The same principle applies.

Because most companies are quick to follow a fad, you can often become a big hero by doing just the opposite.

Suppose you are given the assignment of coming up with new products.

When you observe the winners and losers in the marketing wars, you can see that a large number of successful products are ones that went against the market.

In other words, if everyone is making one type of thing, try making just the opposite.

Lean Cuisine was a big success, so All American Gourmet Company just reversed the concept. Its Budget Gourmet line now has about 15 percent of the frozen entree market.

One reason imported beers did well in the United States was the fact that imports were full-bodied brews in contrast to the lighter American beers. Now along comes Amstel Light to reverse that position.

Like Budget Gourmet, Amstel Light is a big success.

History abounds with businesses built on "going against." When everyone was chasing IBM in mainframes, DEC went small with the minicomputer. In the process Digital Equipment Corporation became the second-largest computer company in the world.

When General Motors was thinking big, Volkswagen thought small. Just about the time the automotive industry gave up on convertibles, Lee Iaccoca brought them back.

So it goes. In an era of jumbo sizes, the hot new food category promises to be the single portion. As hamburger chains move to bigger sit-down restaurants, more of their customers appear to be just driving through.

The moral here is obvious. Just figure a way to do the opposite of what everyone else is doing and you just might find yourself a successful hot new product.

The role of reality

Every marketing plan desperately needs a healthy dose of reality. Yet the temptation to go off into the wild blue yonder is sometimes overwhelming.

The comments around the conference table are more likely to be blue sky rather than brown earth. "Everybody is drinking Perrier." "Nobody smokes anymore." "Domestic cars are dead." You get the picture.

Don't do your thinking around the conference table. It's too easy to be led astray by the fad of the week.

Steak & Ale, the restaurant chain owned by Pillsbury, believed that nobody was eating steak anymore. Think of all those articles in the press about the danger of high cholesterol. So Steak & Ale added shrimp and fish and chicken to the menu. Sales took a dive.

So Steak & Ale promptly returned to its original concept, but the detour into health food destroyed its momentum, which is hard to recover.

Reality is not an exciting concept, which is one reason the business schools don't teach reality. What they do teach is "moving with the market."

Nine times out of ten, the market is just following the latest fad. Next week it will change again.

You can't steer the corporate ship by trying to ride each wave in *The Wall Street Journal* or *The New York*

Times. You steer the ship by trying to catch the long-term tides.

Unfortunately for your planning process, the press usually doesn't see the news value in the long-term trend until it's too late for you to get on board.

4

Narrowing your focus

You've been down to the front immersing yourself in the details. You've been monitoring the trends for any long-term shifts that may influence your markets. Now what do you do?

You narrow your focus.

Throughout history, battles were won because generals were able to concentrate their forces at the decisive point. In other words, they were able to focus their resources on a single sector of a front.

"Keep the forces concentrated in an overpowering mass," says Clausewitz. "The fundamental idea. Always to be aimed at before all and as far as possible."

The battle of Waterloo was won because Wellington was able to bring his Prussian allies into the crucible at a critical time.

The battle of Waterloo was lost because Napoleon was unable to focus on one enemy at a time.

The opposite of human instinct

Focus is a powerful concept to put into practice because it is the exact opposite of human instincts and behavior. A field commander is under pressure to put out a plethora of small fires. So he dispatches a squad here, a company there. When the moment of truth arrives, he no longer has the preponderance of force needed for victory.

So, too, in marketing. Every major company we have analyzed is not fighting a war. It is fighting hundreds of brush fires, diluting its strength and thus ensuring a lack of success when the big opportunity presents itself.

In this sense, human nature follows nature itself. Entropy is what the natural sciences use to measure the degree of disorder in a system. Entropy always increases and available energy diminishes in a closed system such as the universe.

You'll find that the natural human tendencies in a company today are to spread the forces. To find new markets, new products, new applications for existing products. To line-extend, to take advantage of the equity in company and brand names. Diffusion is the order of the day. (Brand leveraging is the latest expression of the diffusion concept.)

Left to its own devices, entropy always increases in a closed system such as a corporation. Available energy decreases and the company becomes vulnerable to competitive attack—on Wall Street as well as on Main Street.

Melting ice cream

Take Häagen-Dazs ice cream parlors, for example. According to *The Wall Street Journal*, they may soon be a thing of the past.

Troubled by melting sales of its 325 Häagen-Dazs shops, owner Pillsbury appears to be considering shutting them down.

The problem? Supermarkets sell the same Häagen-Dazs ice cream for less. How did this happen? Line extension, of course.

The problem is that line extension sounds so sound. "We can take advantage of our premium reputation by selling the same ice cream in two places. The store will create broad awareness and sampling. The supermarkets will generate volume."

Synergism strikes out again. When will companies learn that the road to success is just that? One road and not two or three or six dozen or more. In a word, focus.

In World War II, successful attacks were launched down a single highway, not on a broad front.

Driving off the road

Perhaps the best example of the principle that two roads are not better than one is American Motors.

Does anyone really believe that American Motors wouldn't have been better off over the past decade if it had focused on its money-making Jeep line and dropped its money-losing passenger car line?

Yes, Joseph E. Cappy does. "To be successful in the automotive business," said the American Motors president, "you need two legs. One is the Jeep; the other is passenger cars." (In the world of marketing, the opposite is true. One-leggedness rules.)

The words are in English, but the accent is French. Typical top-down thinking. One wonders whether Renault wanted American Motors to make money or to push Renault passenger cars.

Now that American Motors is no longer with us, what does its new owner, Chrysler, plan to do?

Drop the passenger car line and rename the dealerships "Jeep." Good first step in focusing the company.

Chrysler's second step undermined the first. It introduced a new Eagle line of passenger cars to be sold by Jeep/Eagle dealers.

Back to the mistakes of the past.

If you go down to the front, the dealership itself, you can see the damage done by the split focus. With a single Jeep line to sell, the sales force can be recruited among "believers" in four-wheel-drive, functional, no-frills vehicles. The service force can also be experts in the concept.

With both Jeeps and Eagles to sell, the sales and service forces are split. When the prospect arrives, the salesperson doesn't say, "Welcome to the land of practical, functional four-wheel drive."

The salesperson says, "What is it that you want to buy?"

"We sell everything" is about as effective a strategy as the church that tries to appeal to everybody by having separate Protestant and Catholic services. ("Turn the lights on the Virgin Mary," says the manager. "It's time for the 5 o'clock mass.")

Focusing is illogical

If the benefits are so clear-cut, why don't more companies practice a focused marketing approach?

For one thing, the benefits aren't clear-cut. On the surface, a narrower focus would seem to reduce business.

Consider a shoe store that does 80 percent of its volume in women's shoes and the rest in men's shoes.

If it specialized in women's shoes only, it would seem logical that sales would fall 20 percent.

And they probably would ... if dropping men's shoes were all the store did.

That's why you can't evaluate the effectiveness of a tactic all by itself. You have to turn the tactic into a strategy and then ask yourself, "Will a women's store strategy make my shoe outlet more competitive?"

Nor is this the first question to ask yourself. To turn a tactic into a strategy requires you to think through the entire marketing process.

It's unlikely, for example, that a family shoe store name should be on a women's store. Change the name.

The same thinking should then be applied to all other areas of the store, including models stocked, window displays, pricing, and, of course, advertising.

The tactic is the point of attack and the strategy is the process of organizing the operation to give maximum thrust to the selected tactic.

When we refer to a tactic, of course, we mean a tactic that is competitive in nature. In the shoe store example, we assume that the competition consists of family shoe stores selling both men's and women's shoes. Narrowing the focus means appealing to a smaller market as opposed to your competition.

If the competition is already narrowly focused with separate stores for women and men, then you have to search for another tactic.

Why is a narrow focus superior to a broader focus?

In any given case, a generalist might be superior to a specialist, but the human mind thinks otherwise. The mind thinks the specialist is superior to the generalist.

Would you rather have your double bypass operation conducted by a general practitioner or a heart surgeon?

Would you rather have your Cadillac serviced by the corner gasoline station or the Cadillac dealer that sold you the car?

Do you buy your shoes at a department store or a shoe store? Most people buy their shoes at a shoe store.

The specialist has the upper hand in the mind.

Understanding the issues

You can't start to narrow your focus until you understand the issues involved. What is the problem? What is keeping your business from taking off in the marketplace?

The process requires objectivity and intellectual honesty. Understanding and facing the problems squarely is the key. Too many people want to duck the issues as a means of protecting old corporate decisions and egos.

All too often, marketing people fail to isolate and get basic agreement on their No. 1 problem. They tend to settle on vague, ill-defined problems such as "How do we keep growing at 15 percent per year?" or "How do we improve our return on investment?"

These are not problems. These are goals or objectives expressed in terms of a problem. It's as if you were asking yourself, "How do I get to be CEO?"

You won't find your problem inside the company. You won't even find your problem in the marketplace.

Invariably the problem is in the mind of the customer or prospect. Marketing today is a battle of ideas, not products or services.

Granted, you'll need to think about making physical changes in the product or service. Or perhaps you'll want to change the corporate name. But all these changes come later, after you have sorted out the perceptions that exist in the mind.

If you work for Volkswagen, you have to face the fact that America still thinks VW is a small, inexpensive, reliable car and that this perception cannot be changed.

If you work for Coca-Cola, you have to face the fact that New Coke is a failure and should be put out of its misery so that the main Coke brand can have a focused advertising program. This is true in spite of the fact that taste tests conclusively prove that New Coke tastes better than Coca-Cola Classic.

The perception is the reality.

If you work for Anheuser-Busch, you have to face the fact that things have gone downhill for Michelob ever since the company abandoned its "First Class Is Michelob" strategy.

If you work for General Motors, you have to face the fact that a Cadillac cannot compete with a Mercedes-Benz, even when the Cadillac is an Allanté priced at $56,000.

If you work for Western Union, you have to face the fact that you can't run a twentieth-century business with a nineteenth-century name.

Generally speaking, do people who work for Volkswagen, Coca-Cola, Anheuser-Busch, General Motors, or Western Union believe what we have just said? Probably not. There is a certain illogic to the notion of focusing.

Furthermore, they know the facts. They know the results of product comparisons, taste tests, road tests. They know they have fine products that deserve a larger market share. All they have to do is to change a few perceptions.

Dealing with perceptions

Therein lies one of the major differences between top-down and bottom-up thinking. Changing perceptions is the modus operandi of the traditional top-down marketer.

Dealing with perceptions is the hallmark of a bottom-up marketer.

You deal with perceptions by making changes in the company or its products, not by trying to make changes in the environment. When the boat is leaking, you don't try to drain the lake. You try to fix the boat.

Company people often get their priorities reversed. They believe they have to fall in love with their products or services or names before they can go out and market them: "If I know in my heart that we have a superior product, then I'm certain to find the right words and pictures and strategies to communicate those beliefs to others."

Falling in love with yourself is a dangerous illusion. It muddles your mind and clouds your thinking.

What you're trying to do in bottom-up marketing is not to change minds, but to take advantage of the perceptions that already are there.

To find an opening, you have to seize on a specific and then generalize it. In fact, you have to over-generalize it.

Marketing is a game where the simple idea beats the complex one, where the single idea beats the multiple thrusts.

To see why this is so, go back to the mind of the prospect. How are you going to get inside a mind? By taking one message and endlessly repeating it in different forms? Or by preparing many different messages?

When one message conflicts with another, you compete with yourself. You confuse the prospect. Who are you and what do you stand for? Prospects strongly resist giving any one product or company two different positions.

If you're in charge of a brand, you need the courage to say "no" to the proposition that you can make more money by "extending the line, using your well-known brand name."

Something for nothing

Line extension offers a compelling financial argument as visions of new business dance in management's head.

They see themselves getting something for nothing as they take a "free ride" on the well-known name.

Unfortunately, there is no free lunch, and in time the piper has to be paid. Cases in point:

1. Scott Paper hung the Scott name on so many products (ScotTissue, Scottkins, Scotties, Scot-Towels) that the word "Scott" began to have no meaning on a shopping list. Then along came Mr. Whipple and those tissue squeezers from Charmin who took away Scott's toilet tissue leadership.

2. Sara Lee lost $8 million trying to become a frozen entree as well as a frozen dessert.

3. Xerox lost millions trying to sell Xerox machines that couldn't make copies. (They were computers.)

4. Life Savers tried unsuccessfully to be both a candy and a gum. Then they launched a bubble gum without the Life Savers name. Bubble Yum is an enormous success. It outsells Life Savers candy.

5. Procter & Gamble, one of the last holdouts against line extension, finally succumbed to the siren song and tried Ivory Shampoo and Ivory Conditioner: two products that are going nowhere.

Rolling along with line extensions

We could go on and on but over the years we haven't put a dent in this windmill called line extension. In category after category, everyone has jumped into the pool. Every major beer has launched a "Light" at great expense and negative results when you measure all the results, including the impact on the main brand.

The five major cigarette brands of our youth have expanded to 269 brands today. Most of them are line extensions. And both the beer and cigarette categories are either flat or declining. The result: More expense and less business for each player.

When a product tries to appeal to everybody, it winds up appealing to nobody. Line extension, in all of its varieties, is a self-destructive process. Over the long-term, line extension tends to destroy support for the core product, core benefit, and core concept.

In packaged goods, certain conditions cause line extensions. These line extensions then result in long-term consequences that weaken both brands and categories. Long-term, any category that is heavy in line extension is also a weak category.

There are two conditions that cause companies to line-extend their brands.

1. *Flat or declining markets.* Examples: Beer, cigarettes, coffee, breakfast cereals.

2. *Consumer concerns about ingredients.* Examples: Caffeine, nicotine, sodium, sugar, calories.

To add insult to injury, the product proliferation caused by line extension has led to demands for "slotting fees" from the retailers whose shelf space, like Japanese real estate, is a shrinking commodity.

Furthermore, line extension usually leads to reduced consumer demand for entire product categories.

When you see Hellmann's Light on the shelf, what do you think? There must be an awful lot of calories in mayonnaise. Is that a message Hellmann's wants to communicate?

Trying to become a generalist

Most companies are trying to become generalists. If it weren't so tragic for stockholders and employees, the trend toward being all things to all people would be laughable. (Remember the "TransPacific Airline & Storm Door Company" in the old Bob Newhart routine?)

Make no mistake about it. The conventional wisdom says that the generalist brand is superior to the specialist brand. That's why line extension is the technique of choice in the marketing world today.

We're not talking about mom-and-pop operations. We're talking big companies with big sophisticated marketing departments. Companies like Colgate-Palmolive, for example. Colgate has destroyed the meaning of many of its brands.

Question: What's a Colgate? Is it a toothpaste, a toothbrush, a tooth powder, a bar of soap, a shaving cream, or a dishwashing detergent?

Answer: All of the above.

"Extending brand equity" has become all the rage as companies like Coca-Cola talk about concepts like "Megabrands."

In the name of cost efficiency and trade acceptance, companies are quite willing to turn a "specialist" brand that stands for a certain type of product or idea into a "generalist" brand that represents two, three, or more types of products.

For example, Chevrolet markets a mind-boggling 51 different car models in 12 nameplates, ranging from $5000 Chevettes to $30,000 Corvettes. In addition, Chevrolet markets a line of trucks.

What's a Chevrolet? Chevrolet is a small, large, cheap, expensive car or truck. Chevrolet is the ultimate generalist brand. Whatever you want, Chevrolet has got it.

Maybe that's one reason why Chevrolet recently lost its sales leadership to Ford. (In truth, Ford isn't much better off than Chevrolet. Ford is only slightly less line-extended.)

What line extension does is to erode the brand's basic identity or position in the mind of the customer and prospect.

Line extension and competition

While the long-term erosion of a brand's identity is the effect of a line-extension policy, the real damage is caused by competition.

Actually, line extension or extending the equity of a brand makes a great deal of sense and should be encouraged with only one small provision: No strong competition should be allowed to pursue the business.

Confusion isn't the enemy; competition is.

The sad saga of General Electric in the appliance business demonstrates this point. "General Electric" is a wonderful name. So it was understandable when General Electric used its name on a wide array of products such as refrigerators, washing machines, dishwashers, blenders, irons, and food processors, to name but a few.

Line extension wasn't the problem. The problem was that competition was allowed in and the specialist brands moved to the top in each category.

Cuisinart leads in food processors. Not GE.

Frigidaire leads in refrigerators. Not GE.

Maytag leads in washing machines. Not GE.

Sunbeam leads in irons. Not GE.

Waring leads in blenders. Not GE.

The only kitchen product that General Electric leads in is, what else, electric ranges.

The vulnerability of the generalist

You see, the generalist is always vulnerable. Del Monte is a wonderful generalist name for canned fruit or vegetables. But a "specialist" named Dole leads in pineapple.

Take the case of Kraft. Many people feel that the wide use of the Kraft name is successful line extension at its best.

It might well have been in the absence of competition. But in jellies and jams, when the generalist Kraft name goes to war with specialist Smuckers, the funny-sounding name wins the market share battle, 37 percent to 9 percent.

And the generalist doesn't do any better in the mayonnaise wars. Kraft Real Mayonnaise has an 18 share versus Hellmann's 42 share.

Luckily for Kraft, it happens to have some specialist brands of its own. In fact, its most successful brand in terms of market share is Philadelphia Brand Cream Cheese, a specialist name if we've ever seen one. Over the years, Philadelphia has had about 70 percent of the cream cheese market.

The paradox of line extension

Everyone knows of a line extension that is successful. But the question is not whether the line extension is successful, but what did the competition do? Which leads us to the two principles of line extension.

1. Line extension is good strategy if specialist competition never develops.

2. Line extension is bad strategy if competition strikes back strongly.

So far, history seems to support these two points. For years, Procter & Gamble's Crisco brand was the leading shortening. Then the world turned to vegetable oil. Of course, Procter & Gamble turned to Crisco Oil.

So who is the winner in the vegetable oil war? Wesson, of course.

Time moves on and corn oil appears on the scene. Of course, Wesson keeps up with technology by introducing Wesson Corn Oil.

So who is the big winner in the corn oil melee? That's right, Mazola.

The success of a no-cholesterol corn oil suggests a no-cholesterol corn oil margarine. So Mazola introduces Mazola Corn Oil Margarine.

So who is the winner in the corn oil margarine category? You're right, it's Fleischmann's.

In each case, a winning specialist became a generalist who lost to a specialist.

Lengthening cigarettes

The same story was played out years ago in cigarettes.

In 1937 Pall Mall introduced an 85-mm cigarette, 15 mm longer than the standard brands like Lucky Strike and Camel.

Pall Mall became the specialist in "king-size" cigarettes. It did well too. In 1960 Pall Mall nudged out Camel to become the top-selling cigarette.

Then someone at Pall Mall said, "Why stop here? Let's move up to the 100-mm length." A brilliant idea.

But rather than introduce a new brand, Pall Mall turned its specialist king-size name into a generalist name. In 1965 it introduced Pall Mall Golds, the first 100-mm cigarette.

Shortly thereafter, a specialist named Benson & Hedges arrived with its 100-mm cigarette and rode away with the market. Today Pall Mall 85-mm and 100-mm cigarettes together have only a 3.1 percent market share, while the 100-mm specialist Benson & Hedges has a 4.2 percent market share.

Once again, the specialist beats the generalist.

The opposite of line extension

Focus is the opposite of line extension.

A marketing message is like the blade of a knife. You must sharpen the knife to drive your message into the mind. You blunt the blade when you broaden your selling strategies.

The mathematics of marketing are different from the mathematics of mathematics. In marketing, you increase sales by subtraction, not addition.

To launch a strong marketing attack, you must be prepared to make sacrifices.

The full line, for example, is a luxury for the leader. If you want to compete against the leader, you have to reduce your product line, not expand it.

The power of a narrow focus

First, the specialist can focus on one product, one benefit, one message. This focus enables the marketer to put a sharp point on the message that quickly drives it into the mind.

Some examples: Domino's Pizza can focus on its 30-minute home delivery. Pizza Hut has to talk about both home delivery and sit-down service.

Duracell can focus on long-lasting alkaline batteries. Eveready talks flashlight, heavy-duty, rechargeables, and alkaline batteries. (Recently, the Eveready Energizer alkaline battery became simply the Energizer, a good move on Eveready's part.)

Castrol can focus on its oil for high-performance small engines. Pennzoil and Quaker State are marketed for all types of engines.

Second, the specialist has the ability to be perceived as the expert or the best. Cray is the best in supercomputers. Philadelphia is the best cream cheese. The original, so to speak.

Finally, the specialist can become the "generic" for the category. Xerox became the generic word for copying. "Please Xerox that for me."

Federal Express became the generic word for overnight delivery. "I'll Federal it to you."

3M's Scotch tape became the generic word for cellophane tape. "I'll Scotch-tape it together."

Even though the lawyers hate it, making the brand name a generic is the ultimate weapon in the marketing wars. But it's something only a specialist can do. The generalist can't become a generic.

Nobody ever says, "Get me a beer from the GE."

Focus in colas

The two-brand strategy of Coca-Cola was made to order for archrival Pepsi-Cola.

Nowhere was the two-brand Coca-Cola strategy more vulnerable than in the fountain market. (A supermarket has room for two Cokes; a fast-food operation doesn't.)

"Why settle for a split decision," said a Pepsi trade ad, "when you can go with the clear winner?"

What an opportunity. Pepsi had already won the battle of the supermarkets. But Coke was winning the fountain war with 60 percent of the market compared with Pepsi's 26 percent.

Then Pepsi sprang a leak. It went out and bought Kentucky Fried Chicken (to go along with its Taco Bell and Pizza Hut chains).

"Why subsidize your competition?" gloated the Coca-Cola Company, who promptly persuaded Wendy's to drop the "Choice of a New Generation."

Pepsi-Cola is in trouble with the fast-food industry. It's going to take a lot of smooth talk and hard dollars to keep Pepsi in the fountain game.

Focus in office automation

Xerox can copy anything. Or so it thought as it tried to copy IBM by bringing out a full line of office automation equipment. You'll notice that Team Xerox hasn't won many games recently.

Selling a system instead of a product is the scientific way to spread your forces, and it must be tempting to many companies. However, before you take this approach, go down to the front and make sure your prospects want to buy a system as badly as you want to sell them one.

Most customers don't. Which is why Wang and Harris and other system suppliers are having so many problems.

Focus is the secret ingredient in virtually every successful marketing program. Even mighty IBM can't afford to attack on all fronts at once. The year Big Blue introduced the PC, it spent 73 percent of its advertising budget on its new baby.

MCI stumbles

MCI, the long-distance telephone company, recently announced a $500 million to $700 million fourth-quarter write-off. Furthermore, the company announced it would lay off 2300 of its 16,000 employees.

That's a big loss in dollars as well as people.

The problem at MCI has been one of focus, starting with the ill-conceived launch of MCI Mail.

MCI is a big company, with revenues in the neighborhood of $4 billion a year. But size is relative.

MCI competes with AT&T, a company many times its size. MCI has only a tiny share (5 percent) of the long-distance market.

If you were competing with the giant size of AT&T, would you launch a product that takes on another monster, the U.S. Postal Service?

If any company is going to go into the electronic mail business, it should be AT&T, not MCI.

Not a Goodyear

It sure wasn't for the King of the Road, the Goodyear Tire and Rubber Company.

But tires and rubber weren't the cause of the problem. Oil was. Specifically Goodyear's 1983 purchase of Celeron Corporation, an oil and gas exploration company, for $820 million in stock.

Not only did the oil business distract Goodyear management, but Goodyear's substantial aerospace and motor wheel business took its eyes off the road as well.

Disaster struck Goodyear in the person of Sir James Goldsmith, the British-French investor who turned up with 11.5 percent of the company and offered to buy the rest.

To fend off Sir James, Goodyear's management bought back his stake and 40 million shares from other stockholders. The move more than doubled Goodyear's debt to $5.3 billion, forcing it to put Celeron and the other two subsidiaries on the block.

The Goodyear work force was reduced 5 percent, the research and development budget was cut 10 percent, and the ad budget was slashed. Capital spending was cut back substantially.

What terrible plan did Goldsmith have for Goodyear? "It's a fine, sound business with world-class technology," said Sir James, "but its diversifications have taken it out of focus."

There's that word "focus" again. Shareholder value at Goodyear would be best served by shedding its nontire operations and concentrating on its core business.

Sounds like a good idea to us. Wonder why Goodyear didn't think of it first.

Will Du Pont be next?

The symptoms are the same: a company that has lost its focus.

Like Goodyear, Du Pont's problem is oil. Specifically the 1981 purchase of Conoco for $7.8 billion, a company that now seems to be worth only $5 billion.

What is saving the jobs of Du Pont's management is the size of the bankroll it would take to buy the company. With a market value of almost $21 billion, Du Pont would be a little rich even for Donald Trump.

The Wilmington company hasn't learned to focus. In an effort to reduce its chemical dependency, Du Pont recently bought a number of drug companies, notably the American Critical Care Unit of Baxter Travenol.

Will drugs go the way of oil? That's asking the wrong question.

If you think you know which way a product like drugs will go, then you should buy a drug company's stock, not the drug company itself.

Forget synergism. It's a myth.

Focus in retailing

One industry that demonstrates the enormous advantages of focus is the retail industry.

The big department stores are losing ground to the small specialty shops. In Manhattan alone, three big old-line stores (Gimbels, Ohrbach's, and Alexander's) have announced plans to shut down.

Yet small specialty chains are booming. The Gap and Benetton are two examples that come to mind.

The department store–specialty store battleground is one of the clearest examples of the power of a focused approach. But note that department store sales didn't decline until after the specialty stores moved into the marketplace.

The time to strike the overextended competitor is before the decline sets in, not after. If you wait until the trend is evident, then it probably is too late. Others will have already moved in to establish their positions.

Divorce Dart and Kraft style

You probably read about the divorce of Dart and Kraft after 6 years of corporate marriage. We think this is the first of many such splits in the marketing community.

A new Kraft Inc. will consist of all the food operations of Dart and Kraft plus Duracell.

(Although batteries and groceries don't make a lot of sense, the powers that be at Kraft didn't want to give up the Duracell moneymaker.)

The remaining units (Tupperware, West Bend appliances, Hobart food-service equipment, etc.) will be spun off to shareholders under the Premark International name.

Despite the problems with the Kraft name, we think both halves will do well. (Two focused companies are stronger than one unfocused one.)

Some Wall Street analysts agree. Kurt Wulff of Donaldson, Lufkin & Jenrette argues that smaller corporations concentrating on one business do better than larger "overcapitalized, diversified" companies.

"Investors," says Mr. Wulff, "are supposed to diversify through their portfolios, not through management."

"I'll have a Miller"

No example better illustrates the dangers of losing your focus than the saga of Miller beer.

The logic probably went like this: We have a leading brand of regular beer (Miller High Life), so why don't we expand our share of the market by using our well-known brand name on a light beer (Miller Lite)?

And it worked. Miller Lite now ranks second in beer sales in America. But what happened to Miller High Life, which used to be in second place?

That brand sprang a leak. In 6 years Miller High Life fell from 23.5 million barrels a year to just 9.4 million. This decline happened in spite of the $310 million Miller Brewing spent in the same period advertising the brand.

Let's go down to the front and see why. The best place to start is at your neighborhood bar.

Ask the bartender for a "Miller" and see what you get. Chances are, you'll get a "Miller Lite."

In other words, Miller has made "Miller" mean Lite. Consequently it cannot mean High Life anymore.

In the boardroom Miller can mean anything the chairman wants it to mean. Down at the front, in the mind of the prospect, it's another matter. In an over-communicated, overbranded, overbeered society, you're lucky if your brand can mean one thing. Almost never can it mean two or three things.

Heinz used to be No. 1 in pickles. But then Heinz took advantage of the equity in the brand name and introduced Heinz ketchup. Very successfully, too.

Along the way, of course, Heinz lost its pickle leadership to Vlasic.

It figures. Vlasic means pickles. Heinz means ketchup.

5

Finding your tactic

You can narrow your focus and monitor the trends only for so long. Sooner or later you'll have to select a competitive mental angle to develop into a strategy.

Actually, you might think through the process several times: Choose one tactic and carry it to a logical conclusion; then discard that tactic and try another.

There are some principles to keep in mind.

Your tactic should not be company-oriented

This is top-down marketing at its worst—selecting a tactic to use because it meets the strategic needs of the corporation.

Xerox bought a computer company (Scientific Data Systems) because it fit their strategic plans to offer their customers an automated office. It was a billion-dollar mistake. Customers already had a plethora of computer companies to choose from: IBM, Digital Equipment, and Wang, to name a few.

Nine out of ten new products are introduced to fill a void in the company's line, not to fill a void in the marketplace. Maybe that's why nine out of ten new products are also failures.

A company focus is wrong. It might win you Brownie points inside the organization, but it can cause disastrous results on the outside.

Your tactic should not be customer-oriented

The great myth of marketing is that "serving the customer" is the name of the game.

Many marketing people live in a dream world. They believe in the fantasy of the virgin market. This is the belief that marketing is a two-player game involving just the company and the customer.

In this fantasy, a company develops a product or service designed to appeal to consumer needs and wants and then uses marketing to harvest the crop.

There are no virgin markets. The reality of marketing is that a market consists of consumers strongly or weakly held by a range of competitors.

A marketing campaign consists, therefore, of holding onto your customers while at the same time attempting to take customers away from your competitors.

What about a new product? Surely there is a lot of virgin territory when you introduce a new product.

Not true. What was the market for videocassette recorders before Sony introduced the Betamax?

Zero. Of course, Sony defined its potential market as the owners of television sets, but there was no guarantee that any of them would buy a VCR.

In spite of all the talk about appealing to the needs and wants of the virgin market, most marketers would rather launch products aimed at existing markets and against entrenched competitors.

The special case of flanking

We define flanking as the introduction of a new product with a significant difference. A typical flanking move is at the high or low end from a price point of view.

Mercedes-Benz, for example, flanked Cadillac at the high end. Volkswagen flanked Chevrolet at the low end.

And Orville Redenbacher Gourmet Popping Corn flanked Jolly Time at the high end. Flanking moves can be very effective, yet many marketers resist them.

What's the market for a high-priced popcorn? Zero, of course, before Orville Redenbacher.

You can't have it both ways. You can't enjoy the advantage of operating against virgin territory and still have the benefit of a defined market.

Your tactic should be competitor-oriented

Not too long ago Delta decided to offer a "triple-mileage" bonus to members (and new members) of its frequent flier club.

It seemed like a good idea, bound to attract a lot of new business for Delta. It did, but the new program also attracted American, United, Pan Am, TWA, and Eastern. In fact, all of Delta's competitors jumped in and offered the same bonus deal. Nobody benefits except the frequent flier.

When Burger King launched its "broiling, not frying" campaign, McDonald's didn't rip out all the fryers in its restaurants and put in broilers. It would have been enormously expensive to do so.

Triple mileage is not a competitor-oriented tactic, because it can be quickly copied.

Speed is an important consideration. If a competitor cannot copy your tactic quickly, then you have the time to preempt the idea in the mind.

Most airline passengers don't know that Delta pioneered the triple mileage idea. Delta didn't have enough time to establish the concept before the competition moved in.

"Broiling, not frying" is a good competitor-oriented tactic because it cannot be copied quickly. Nor can it be copied economically.

When Michelin attacked the U.S. market with the radial-ply tire, it put Goodyear and Firestone on the defensive for many years to come. Even if the big wheels in the U.S. tire industry were willing to invest the money in radial-tire facilities, it would take years to get their production lines running.

The only tactic worth considering is the tactic that puts the knife into the competition. Tactics that just offer the customer some incentive to purchase also offer the competition some incentive to copy.

Yet most marketing programs involve coupons, rebates, in-store promotions, and a variety of deals. The ones that don't work cost you money. The ones that do work buy you the sincerest form of flattery; your competitors copy you.

You can't win by pleasing the consumer. Forget the deals. What would please the consumer most is your giving the product away.

On the other hand, a tactic that displeases one or more of your competitors is bound to be good for your business.

Avoid the "flavor of the month" tactic

A common tactic you should try to avoid is "more choice." Some companies have based entire marketing programs on a "flavor of the month" philosophy.

Who is most likely to buy that hot new flavor or line extension? Your existing customers, of course. Not your competitors' customers. Even if the new flavor did have some competitor-oriented impact, guess who would be quick to copy? Your competitors would.

You can't preempt a flavor. Who invented strawberry ice cream? Who knows? A new flavor is not in the same category as xerography.

Furthermore, more choice for the consumer also comes with built-in problems. One is confusion. Which flavor do I buy? The second is availability. The more flavors the product comes in, the more likely the flavor that any one customer wants will be out of stock.

When Coke was Coke, it was unthinkable that a supermarket would be out of Coca-Cola.

Now that Coke is New, Classic, Diet, Cherry, Diet Cherry, Caffeine-Free, and Diet Caffeine-Free, it's a lot more likely that your supermarket will be out of stock of the Coke you want to buy.

More choice complicates the buying decision for many products. Does the fact that Chevrolet offers 10 models (in a bewildering array of body styles and engine options) make it any easier to buy a Chevrolet?

General Motors used to brag that when all the options had been combined in every conceivable way, you could order a million different Chevrolets.

More than half the new Chevrolets bought are bought off the dealers' showroom floor with the buyers' choices limited to the undercoating and the wax finish. (Yes or no.)

When you are your own competitor

When you dominate the category, sometimes you are your own competitor. In this case, you should launch products that attack yourself. Skillfully done, you can have your cake and eat it too.

Gillette is the best example. It owned the single-blade razor market with the Blue Blade.

Then Gillette attacked itelf with the Trac II. "Two blades shave better than one," said the Trac II ads.

The one blade that the two-bladed razor shaved better than was Gillette's own Blue Blade.

Then Gillette introduced Atra, the first adjustable two-bladed razor. "Are you shaving with a fixed two-bladed razor?" said the Atra ads in a pointed reference to its own Trac II product.

Market shares in excess of 50 percent of the market usually rely on a variation of the Gillette multiple-brand strategy.

The day Gillette introduced Trac II, the company had 55 percent of the wet-shaving market. Today Gillette has almost two-thirds of the market, a considerable accomplishment in the face of ferocious competition from Schick, Bic, Wilkinson, and others.

Don't confuse the Gillette tactics with Coca-Cola's line extensions. The seven Coke flavors are all marketed under the Coca-Cola name, causing confusion in the mind of the prospect.

Each Gillette product, especially the key Trac II and Atra products, has its own brand name, reducing the confusion.

It's true, of course, that both Trac II and Atra carry the word "Gillette" in a secondary-size type on the package. (The Gillette name serves a function in the distribution process. For one thing, it tells the trade where to reorder.)

In this respect, it's like the GM name on a Chevrolet. The primary brand name is still Chevrolet.

Simple is better than complex

Although the human species admires complexity, most prospects rarely take the time to try to figure everything out.

Simple ideas are easier to implement and prospects find them easier to understand.

All too often, companies try to impress prospects with a dazzling array of complexity rather than sell them the simple ideas they want to buy.

Several years ago, in an effort to restore a sagging reputation in the office systems market, Xerox introduced an array of new products in highly publicized waves. Xerox rented the Vivian Beaumont Theatre at New York's Lincoln Center and loaded the stage with a complex array of office systems. It was an attempt to dazzle with technology.

The result was a presentation that boggled the mind but failed to dazzle the press or its prospects. It was just too complex to deal with.

Why do the Xeroxes of this world do these things? Typical top-down thinking. They wanted to impress the marketplace with the concept that Xerox was going to be a major player in the office information business.

Buried in this array of products was a new laser printer that was also a copier. (The Laser CP.)

This simple tactic, a computer printer that is also a copier, would have worked a lot better alone than the complex array of products from printers to computers that Xerox actually introduced.

A good example of the value of simplicity is the radio station that was looking for a way to differentiate itself from its competitors. It found that people like to get the latest weather as quickly as possible, so it chose the tactic of increasing the number of weather reports during each broadcast hour.

Then the station went on television and promoted the idea of more frequent, up-to-the-minute reports.

It worked. It breezed by its competition with a tactic that couldn't have been any simpler.

Why didn't its competitors copy the tactic? They could have, of course, but the station that does it first always has the advantage if it moves rapidly enough to preempt the idea in the mind.

Different but not necessarily better

When you're up against a clearly superior product, you can forget about marketing.

Take the 914 plain-paper copier. It was clearly superior to the thermography machines from 3M and Kodak. As expected, Thermofax and Verifax were wiped out. (Just as jet planes wiped out piston-engine planes in the airline market.) It was like a Mike Tyson fight. It took place in a ring, but it wasn't boxing.

Learning the principles of marketing is useless if you have to compete with xerography and your product is based on thermography.

Learning the principles of warfare won't help very much either if you are fighting an enemy which has nuclear bombs ... and you don't.

Fortunately, the clearly superior product happens very seldom. Is a BMW better than a Volvo? Who is to say? They are different, however.

Volvo has built its strategy around "durability," using the tactic of stacking six cars on top of one another. BMW has built its strategy around "the ultimate driving machine."

The competitor that BMW took on was Mercedes-Benz. Both were expensive German cars, but Mercedes had arrived first and preempted the "engineering" position.

Should BMW have taken on its Teutonic rivals with a better engineering approach? Could it have toppled Mercedes with a campaign based on BMW's patented triple-hemispheric, swirl-action combustion chambers?

"Betterness" is a subjective concept. That's why it's always better to avoid attacking a competitor where the competitor is strong.

What's the difference between a BMW and a Mercedes? The difference is not in the car; it's in the driver. The older driver preferred the established, more expensive Mercedes. The younger driver preferred the newer, less expensive BMW.

One reason younger drivers prefer the BMW is because older drivers prefer the Mercedes. (This is also the reason why the Pepsi Generation strategy is so effective.)

What's the essential characteristic of younger drivers? They drive faster. (Go down to the front, at the nearest "Stoplight Grand Prix," and check it out.)

Let Mercedes-Benz have engineering. BMW became a big success by exploiting the driving position.

Recently BMW moved into Mercedes territory by introducing its 7-Series models. BMW is starting to lose its focus, a move that could undermine its entire product line.

A concept is better than a product

Marketing today is a battle of concepts, not products. The true measure of a tactic is whether or not you have a concept or idea to drive your business. As Walter Wriston said, "Ideas are the new currency in corporate America."

The computer industry is a good example of the power of a concept. For the first time in its life, IBM has competitors that are giving it trouble in the office market. DEC has become especially troublesome with its "single operating system" approach to selling minicomputers.

At the other end of the scale, Apple has begun to make progress with a concept called "desktop publishing." This idea has captured the imagination of many users and is helping to sell a lot of Macintosh computers into the land of the Fortunate 1000.

If you were a marketing manager at IBM, what would you do about this new-found competition?

Well, so far it has pursued the better-product, better-sales-effort, breakthrough-advertising approach to regaining control of a market it had dominated.

No one does the more-is-more approach better than IBM. (It helps to have IBM's resources.)

It introduced not one, not two, but a whole new generation of PCs, the Personal System/2. It also started to advertise not one, not two, but five different midrange computer systems.

It dramatically beefed up its sales force, sending thousands more salespeople into the field. Even its CEO, John Akers, got into the act as he met with customer groups, promising them that IBM would listen better to their suggestions and complaints.

Not to be outdone, the IBM advertising folks checked in with some breakthrough advertising.

Charlie Chaplin was shown the door and was replaced by not one, not two, but the entire cast from M.A.S.H., including Alan Alda (who is rumored to have a $10 million contract).

So far all this effort hasn't slowed DEC or Apple down one bit as they continue to show important gains in the office market.

And IBM's introduction of "personal publishing" appears to have gone all but unnoticed as companies continue to purchase Apple's "desktop publishing" in a big way.

Despite all of IBM's power and strength, it has only one move to make—an obvious one.

But first, IBM has to recognize the nature of the battle. From the very outset, the computer wars have been a battle of ideas and concepts.

IBM first introduced the concept of "data processing" with mainframe computers. DEC countered the big computer idea with the concept of a "minicomputer" that allowed you to do "office processing."

Apple then rode the concept of the "personal computer" for the home and the school. IBM laid claim to the "office" personal computer.

Other players built businesses around concepts. Wang did well with "word processing." Cray prospered with "supercomputers." Tandem took off with its "dual processing" systems. Compaq did well with small "portable computers."

Each of the big winners had one thing in common: they had an idea or concept to ride.

IBM failed to read computer history. In recent years it has moved away from a concept approach. IBM has been using a product strategy in the marketplace as it introduced more and more boxes.

Look at IBM's advertising and you can see its strategy. IBM advertising features an array of products and the offer of "whatever you want, we've got it." IBM's basic pitch to customers is "We'll work out what's best for you."

The weakness of this approach is that customers often don't know what they want, especially in a high-technology category. Customers buy what they think they should have. And if they think they should have concepts like a "single operating system" or "desktop publishing," DEC and Apple get the business.

The only move open to IBM is to fight these concepts with a concept of its own.

A concept for paper

A concept like "desktop publishing" sometimes creates a spinoff market for other products or services.

Material that was once printed outside a company can now be produced right at the desktop. Reports and documents that took days can now be produced in hours.

Let's say you're a bright young marketing person in a big paper company that has noticed this trend. Your marching orders from the top are to launch a new mill brand of business paper.

Unfortunately, there are some difficulties with these orders because there is a long line of competitors already in the market with mill brands. Companies like

Hammermill, Nekoosa, Boise Cascade, Champion, and Mead.

Paper merchants sell most of this paper. So your starting point in search of a tactic should be to find out what's selling with the merchants. What you discover is that their "private brand" paper is selling better than the mill's paper.

But all the news isn't bad. You discover that some large users who are into electronic publishing are ordering a better grade of offset printing paper for their machines.

Eureka! Now that's an interesting competitive mental angle. Launch a high-end flanking brand. (Orville Redenbacher Gourmet Paper for the laser printer.)

This brand will have superior brightness and opacity and will be targeted for use with important documents.

Basically, you need to encourage the user to consider stocking two types of business machine paper. One for everyday internal work. And one for external work.

You've got your work cut out for you, but you've got a concept to ride which should take you a lot further than selling paper on price and delivery.

You can't have the honey without the flies

It was a character in Machiavelli's *La Mandragola* who said, "You can't have the honey without the flies." With every positive competitive mental angle comes a negative.

It's as important to promote the negative as the positive. The negative is what gives your tactic its credibility.

Department stores have found that a sale is more effective when the goods are promoted as "seconds" or "irregulars." These words give the prospect a reason for the low price. (Stores have been known to throw in the "firsts" to keep the sale of seconds running longer.)

A discount store will often call itself a "factory outlet" for exactly the same reason. Or it might deliberately create a warehouse feeling with cheap tables and fixtures.

When Charles Schwab launched his discount brokerage firm, he stressed the fact that his company had no sales representatives or account executives to give you advice. No one from Charles Schwab would ever call you to try to sell you anything. (Skillfully done, promoting a negative in this way can often make it sound like a positive.)

As the Charles Schwab ads say, "Where's the catch? What do I give up to get these big commission discounts?"

"Well, there's only one catch and here it is: *We don't give you investment advice.*"

It might sound terrific to say, "We have everything our competitors have ... at a lower price." But where's the catch?

That's exactly what your prospects are going to say. That's why, for credibility reasons, you must advertise the catch as well as the promise.

What does a low price say about a product? Exactly. (Try selling a gold Rolex watch on the streets of New York for $50 and you'll see what the low price says. Either the watch is phony or it's stolen or both.)

"The 1970 Volkswagen Beetle will stay ugly longer." This was a powerful statement because it was psychologically sound. When you admit a negative, the prospect is inclined to give you the positive.

What the Volkswagen buyers gave up was styling. What they got in return was reliability.

"Made in Korea" is the negative that gives validity to the low price of the Hyundai Excel. It answers the question, "How can the Excel be any good if its price is so low?"

"The costliest perfume in the world"

Joy perfume uses that slogan. As a matter of fact, high price is the catch that gives credibility to a quality tactic.

What does a high price say about the product? That's right. The product is worth a lot. In essence, the high price becomes an inherent benefit of the product itself. (This is one of the powerful motivating factors in the success of many high-end flanking moves. Mercedes-Benz automobiles, Absolut vodka, Grey Poupon mustard, to name three examples.)

A case in point is Absolut vodka. Priced 50 percent higher than Smirnoff, Absolut has been growing at an astounding rate. In four years, sales quadrupled. Absolut now ranks fourth in U.S. vodka sales, selling more than a million cases a year. (Absolut is not a fad because total vodka sales have been moving up only moderately.)

If high price is a benefit for any product that's not a commodity, then why not price every product as high as possible? There are a lot of people out there who have more dollars than sense.

The reason is the inverse relationship between price and demand. The higher the price, the lower the demand.

Rolls-Royce automobiles are "worth more" because they are high in price. Yet very few are sold, because most people can't afford them.

You have to balance price with demand. You can make a lot more money selling a million low-price Fords than a thousand high-price Rolls-Royces.

Price is only one of the tactical elements to look at. There are many others to consider. You might find a competitive mental angle based on large size in a category loaded with small products.

It could be a masculine product in a category dominated by feminine brands.

Or you could find a tactic in small size as Sony did. Or in a feminine brand as Virginia Slims did.

You won't find a competitive idea inside your own organization, however. You have to go down to the front to look for one.

6

Finding a tactic to fight drug abuse

It's very difficult to run a communications program that tries to stop the flow of cocaine, marijuana, and other illegal drugs into America.

Millions of Americans want to consume drugs. We've repeatedly pointed out the difficulty of trying to change people's minds.

How do you "reduce the demand" for drugs? The trick is to find a way to take advantage of perceptions already lurking in the minds of drug users.

You're in charge

Put on your marketing hat. You've just received a call from the new President. You're to head up a new government-sponsored communications program to replace Nancy Reagan's "Say No to Drugs" campaign, a program that appears to have had little impact on reducing demand. Obviously, some changes are called for if progress is to be made.

And progress is desperately needed.

After years of effort and billions of dollars spent in law enforcement, it would appear there is only one long-term way to decrease the usage and sale of drugs in America: you have to find a way to decrease demand.

Decreasing supply only increases the price and the profit potential for suppliers willing to take the risks. Since the product cost is so low and the return so high, experience shows that there is no effective way, outside of legalizing drugs, that will force illegal drug suppliers out of business. For every drug dealer you shut down, two will open up.

So the question is, "What is the best tactic to use to decrease demand?"

Monitoring the trends

Let's start with a quick monitoring of the trends in substance abuse. As in any problem, you don't always just focus on the product at hand. You try to get a feeling for the entire category.

In this case, the smoking of cigarettes offers important parallels in looking for the answer to the problem of drug consumption.

Like drugs, cigarettes introduce a foreign substance into the body. They can be addictive, and it is widely accepted that they are bad for you. In fact, they are reported to kill 50 times as many Americans as drugs do.

The main differences between cigarettes and drugs are that cigarettes are legal as well as an important revenue source for the government.

As a result, just about everyone knows that cigarettes are bad for you, yet cigarette sales have not shown a steep decline. (To be honest, demand has turned down. Today, cigarettes kill only 48 times as many Americans as drugs do.)

It would appear that the educational approach that presents the health hazards of smoking has failed to overcome the image enhancement that cigarette companies have promised in their advertising. Eliminating cigarettes from broadcast advertising has hurt the industry's ability to launch new brands, but the message still gets through via a wide array of media still available to cigarette advertisers.

"Bad for you" doesn't work

On the basis of the cigarette lesson, you can probably surmise that an educational "bad for you" approach might not be a good tactic to dramatically reduce demand if drugs continue to be perceived as "in." This is probably why the "Say No" program hasn't had the desired effect.

The same can be said for the advertising industry's $500 million effort that for the most part also says "bad for you" in a number of different ways.

What this monitoring of the cigarette experience shows you is that the traditional "top-down" approach of telling people what's bad for them rarely works. In other words, it's time to shift the battlefield.

"In" versus "out"

What appears to be more of an influence on consumption of a product is its social message. (Before World War II every star in a Hollywood movie smoked. Today few smoke on film.)

This insight offers an opportunity. Unlike cigarette manufacturers, drug producers and sellers cannot use advertising to promote a fashionable image for their drugs. On the other hand, government *can* use advertising to make drugs less and less fashionable to use.

If America runs true to form, this will dramatically reduce demand. When a product is "out" in America, it doesn't sell.

Now to your important decision: What concept can you use to begin to make drugs unfashionable?

The tactical idea

When you study the situation, one obvious idea jumps out as a tactic to employ. It has been widely demonstrated that drug use is a one-way street. Heavy users are in danger of losing their jobs, losing their friends, losing their families, losing their self-esteem, losing their freedom, and eventually losing their lives.

What this sets up is a simple play on words that can be a two-edged sword against the drug dealers. One that points out the bad things that drugs can do to you while presenting them in the context of a social image.

The idea: Drugs are for losers.

If the perception that "Drugs are for losers" can be established, a mortal blow at demand will be struck. If

America disdains anything, it's a loser. Underdogs are acceptable, but winners are what America admires most and what everyone aspires to.

Turning a tactic into a strategy

Now it's time for you to turn your tactical idea into a national strategy by figuring out who should deliver this message to America.

The natural choice is to have ex-drug users or relatives of users tell their sad and moving stories. The natural medium is television with its emotional and personal impact.

Celebrities and sports stars who have had publicized drug problems could be asked to participate in this program. Examples could be comedian Richard Pryor talking about how he almost lost his career, ex-baseball-star Denny McLain talking about how he went to jail and lost his freedom, John Belushi's wife talking about how her husband lost his life.

At the end of every commercial, the subject would look in the camera and say "Drugs are for losers." As more and more famous and infamous people deliver that message, America will begin to see that drugs take you down, not up.

When this happens, the demand for drugs will start down and the drug business will become a lot less profitable. This is bound to make organized crime think twice about the risk/return ratio in the drug business.

7

Building your strategy

It's time to turn your tactic into a strategy.

The Little Caesars' pizza takeout chain developed a two-for-one sale. This was the tactic—the competitive mental angle—it selected to fight Pizza Hut, Godfather's, and the other chains.

Normally sales are limited in time. They may last a day, a week, a month. They are used to stimulate trial. Give prospects a good deal to try the product and maybe some of them will become long-term customers at regular prices.

That's normally the fate of most tactics. They come and they go like the tide.

Little Caesars', however, turned the tactic into a strategy by having a continuous two-for-one promotion.

The key concept is "continuous." To turn a tactic into a strategy, you must add the ingredient of time. You must find a way to incorporate the tactic into the fabric of organization and make it the company's key strategic concept, or reason for being.

"Two-for-one," the Little Caesars' slogan, became a coherent marketing direction. Little Caesars' became one of the most successful pizza chains with this simple strategy.

Most of the other pizza chains have been forced to add a two-for-one deal to their menus. These competitive responses, however, have been at the tactical level only. Pizza Hut, for example, can't afford to turn the chain into a two-for-one operation. It wouldn't be able to pay for its prime locations, its fancy seating, the salaries of waiters and waitresses, etc.

Little Caesars', of course, is a takeout-only chain. To make the two-for-one concept work over an extended period of time, it has to keep its focus on low-cost locations and limited service.

The other pizza chain that successfully turned a tactic into a strategy is Domino's. The tactic that drives the Domino's business is home delivery of pizza in 30 minutes or less.

The traditional top-down process asks the questions in the "logical" order: (1) what food items do we want to sell and (2) how long would it take to deliver them?

The bottom-up process is just the reverse. Focusing on a tactic turns the planning process upside down. What food items can we sell to fit into the 30-minute delivery cycle?

To meet the guarantee, Domino's reduced the number of pizza sizes to two and cut the number of toppings to six. They sell just one beverage, a cola.

The essence of turning a tactic into a strategy is in making changes in the company or the product, not in trying to change the environment.

The tactic is your competitive angle. Be it "two-for-one" or "30-minute delivery" or whatever. When you turn your tactic into a strategy, the challenge is to maintain that single-minded clarity over an extended period of time. It's not easy. The pressure is to modify the strategy to incorporate other products or ideas. That weakens and dilutes the power of a coherent marketing direction.

Most companies start with the strategy. They decide what they want to do and then they try to determine the tactics necessary to achieve their strategic goals.

Exxon wanted to sell office automation systems but prospects didn't want to buy office systems from Exxon. They wanted to buy them from IBM and DEC.

No problem. Exxon is a rich oil company with revenues exceeding IBM and DEC combined. Exxon would mount a multimillion-dollar advertising campaign and convince prospects of the quality of Exxon's products and the sincerity of its purpose.

Team Exxon struck out. You can't change the marketplace. You have to change yourself to get in sync with what the market wants to buy, and even more important, whom it wants to buy from.

In other words, you have to first find a tactic that will work. Massive advertising programs are no substitute for a simple effective tactic.

A coherent marketing direction

When you start with a single tactic and turn it into a strategy, you restrict yourself to a single marketing move. The process results in a coherent marketing direction.

The bottom-up marketing process rules out many popular strategies. Strategies that are too general, too diverse, too difficult to execute are automatically excluded when you think from the bottom up.

Most corporate strategies are not grounded in reality. They are not executable in any true sense of the word.

"We want to be the leader in the luxury car market" seems to be the Cadillac strategy. This kind of thinking leads to a full line of high-end vehicles, including the Cimarron and the Allanté, both of which are strategic disasters because they are not tactically sound.

Time and again the overly broad, overly optimistic, overly general strategy leads to a morass of tactical errors. Yet who pays the price when the strategy is wrong?

Usually it's not the general who devised the strategy. It's the field commanders assigned to execute the strategy tactically who usually get it in the neck.

Ronald Reagan wasn't indicted for his Iran/Contra strategy.

But the men who executed the tactics weren't so lucky. Oliver North, John Poindexter, Richard Secord, and Albert Hakim were indicted.

The power of the single move

When you work from the bottom up, you are certain to wind up with one tactic and a single strategy. In other words, you force yourself to concentrate on a single, powerful marketing move.

This is the most important consequence of a bottom-up approach. It's the essence of good marketing thinking.

When you work from the top down, when you start with a strategy and then develop the tactics, you invariably wind up with many different tactics.

Most of the tactics, of course, turn out to be ineffective. How could they be otherwise? They were not selected because they would work; they were selected to "support" the strategy.

Furthermore, the existence of many different tactics makes the total marketing program incoherent and therefore ineffective.

Why do marketing people think two moves are better than one? Would a boxer throw both his left and his right hand at the same time?

Would a military general attack at every point on the front at the same time? Never.

Would a marketing general attack all markets with all products at the same time? Yes, they do it all the time, but never very effectively.

Companies that believe in flailing away simultaneously on all fronts usually also believe in the 12- or 16-hour day.

Their religion says that trying harder is the secret of success. (In case you haven't noticed, Hertz is still in front of Avis by a big margin.)

Yet hope springs eternal for many 12-hour marketing executives. They cling to the belief that their people are somehow better, and that with just a little more effort or with a little more product improvement or with some better advertising, truth will out and a competitor will be vanquished.

Their strategy often consists of trying to do the same as the leader in the category but only a little better. It's like a general saying that all we have to do is fight a little harder wherever we choose to fight and everything will work out.

Trying harder is not the secret of marketing success.

History says it's just the opposite. Successful generals study the situation and look for that one bold stroke that is least expected by the enemy. Finding one is difficult. Finding more than one is usually impossible.

Military strategist and author B. H. Liddell Hart calls this bold stroke "the line of least expectation."

The Allied invasion came at Normandy, a place whose tide and rocky shore the Germans felt would be an unlikely choice for a landing of any scale.

So it is in marketing. There is often only one place where a competitor is vulnerable. And that place should be the focus of the entire invading force. That is the tactic that you are looking for to develop into a strategy.

When you find it, you must build your strategy from the bottom up. You must take that tactic and commit the resources of your entire company in the campaign to exploit it.

Driving around General Motors

The automobile industry is an interesting case in point. For years, the leader's main strength was in the middle of the line.

With brands like Chevrolet, Pontiac, Oldsmobile, Buick, and Cadillac, General Motors easily beat back frontal assaults by Ford, Chrysler, and American Motors. The Edsel fiasco is a typical example.

GM's dominance became legendary.

What works in marketing is the same thing that works in the military: the unexpected tactic.

Hannibal came over the Alps, a route that was deemed impossible to scale. Hitler came around the Maginot Line and sent his panzer divisions through the Ardennes, terrain the French generals thought impossible to traverse with tanks. (As a matter of fact, he did it twice. Once in the Battle of France and once again in the Battle of the Bulge.)

Since World War II, there have been two strong moves made against GM. Both were moves around the GM Maginot Line.

The Japanese came at the low end with small cars like Toyota, Datsun, and Honda.

The Germans came at the high end with super-premium cars like Mercedes and BMW. History points to the fact that there were no other moves to be made in terms of gaining a substantial amount of ground from General Motors.

With the success of the Japanese and German attacks, GM was under pressure to commit resources in an attempt to shore up the bottom and top of its lines.

In an effort to save money and maintain its profits, GM made the fateful decision to build many of its mid-range cars using the same body style. This was a typical top-down strategic decision. Suddenly, no one could tell a Chevrolet from a Pontiac or a Buick or an Oldsmobile. They all looked alike.

This dramatically weakened GM in the middle and opened up a move for Ford as it broke through with the European-styled Taurus and Sable models.

When you look at the General Motors situation from the bottom up, the tactical solution to the problem is obvious. GM needs a different name and a different look in each price category.

When you build that tactic into a strategy, you wind up with Alfred P. Sloan's original concept for General Motors. What Sloan developed, Smith should not have changed.

"We use the General Motors system," you might be thinking. "We have a different product for each price category. We just don't give our products a different name. We use the corporate name because it's more efficient to do it that way. How do we achieve the market penetration of a GM?"

You don't. Your strategy isn't built from the bottom up. It isn't based on a competitive mental angle, a tactic that will work.

It seems like such a small point: a different name for each product. But all tactics are small points.

If the strategy is a hammer, the tactic is a nail. Note that the penetration is accomplished by the nail, not by the hammer.

You can have the world's most powerful hammer (i.e., the strategy) but the marketing program isn't going to work if it isn't hitting the right nail (i.e., the tactic.)

All the strategic power of General Motors isn't going to put a dent in BMW with a product called Buick Reatta. The tactic is wrong.

"It's just a name," you might be thinking. "It's a small thing."

You're right on both counts. Tactics are small things which you build into strategies which are big things. It's a fascinating, upside-down process that can produce fabulous marketing successes.

GM is history. That's an easy call to make.

The real problem at Coca-Cola

Let's look at the continuing battle between Coca-Cola and Pepsi-Cola. What can Coke do to break out of its costly trench warfare with Pepsi?

At present, Coca-Cola is fighting a two-front battle with Classic and New Coke. While Classic has regained most of its original strength, New Coke (the Edsel from Atlanta) is barely hanging on.

Just to illustrate how "barely," the two brands combined were in the fall of 1988 still a share point below where Coke was in 1983, when the whole mess began.

Since then, Coke has been through an endless parade of tactical ideas trying to make headway against Pepsi-Cola's youth-oriented "Pepsi Generation."

Every year you've seen a different slogan for Coca-Cola: "We have a taste for you." "The real choice." "Catch the wave." "Red, white, and you." "You can't beat the feeling." (In comparison, the "Pepsi Generation" is 25 years old.)

None of Coke's tactical ideas have caught on. You can count on the parade of ideas to continue for some time in the future.

Any day now, Coke's corps commanders will parade into an Atlanta conference room and paper the wall with yet another new set of slogans. Coke's top management will then sit around and discuss the latest batch of creative moves until they agree on their next effort, which we predict will meet the same fate as such immortal lines as "We have a taste for you."

Coca-Cola can't find the answer to its problem in Atlanta. It has to go down to the front.

When you look in the mind of the prospect, there is only one move for Coke to make. The move is in two parts. One is a step backwards, the other a step forward.

First of all, the company has to bite the bullet and drop New Coke. Not because it's a loser or an embarrassment, but because the existence of New Coke effectively blocks Coke from using the tactical advantage it has in the prospect's mind.

With New Coke safely tucked away in the archives, Coke would be able to bring back the concept of the "Real Thing." (When you think of a Coca-Cola, don't you think of it as being the real thing?)

Having brought back this concept (by popular demand), Coke is in a position to turn it against the "Pepsi Generation" and blow Pepsi-Cola out of the refrigerator.

To pull the trigger, all Coke has to do is to go on television and say to the Pepsi Generation: "All right, kids, we're not going to push you. But when you're ready for the Real Thing, we've got it for you."

That would be the beginning of the end of the Pepsi Generation. As any parent will tell you, no kid north of ten years old wants an imitation. They want the real thing ... in baseball bats, Barbie dolls, blue jeans, sneakers, and colas.

Change the company, not the market

The Coca-Cola situation illustrates one of the key aspects of bottom-up marketing. In building a tactic into a strategy, you have to be prepared to make changes in the product and the company. You can't force change on the marketplace.

A marketing tactic is a mental angle. It has to work in the mind. The one unshakable idea that lurks in the mind is that Coca-Cola is the "real thing." Coke ought to drop New Coke because it undermines that powerful tactical idea.

Yet ego often gets in the way. Dropping New Coke will be an admission to the business community that Coca-Cola made a mistake. And the folks in Atlanta know that their avowed enemy, Pepsi-Cola, will be among the first to point it out. And it won't be in the form of a letter or a phone call. It will probably be in the form of full-page, nationwide newspaper ads.

Coke should cut its losses. "Defending yesterday," says Peter Drucker, "is far more risky than making tomorrow."

Sometimes an excellent strategy can be waylaid by the addition of one element that undercuts the tactical power of the concept.

Say you work for the Holiday Corporation and you've worked out the tactic and the strategy for a new kind of hotel to compete with Marriott and Hyatt. And you've come up with a wonderful high-end name, Crowne Plaza. Not bad.

But lo and behold, the CEO or some of his henchmen at Holiday want to hang the corporate name on it and make it "Holiday Inn Crowne Plaza."

Oops, there goes your high-end idea. The Crowne Plaza name gets dragged down to the Holiday Inn level.

Management might even agree that this approach reduces the tactical power of the high-end marketing campaign. Strategy first, tactics second. You just have to try harder.

They justify their decision by quoting the corporate strategy document, "We will leverage our strength by using the Holiday Inn name on all of our properties."

It usually does no good to protest these kinds of decisions. "That's a tactical detail," says Holiday management. "With a little extra effort you can work around it."

Not true. The tactic dictates the strategy. The tactical side of a marketing battle consists of details. If the nail isn't straight, the battle is lost.

When building a strategy, you cannot let corporate considerations alter the tactic. Sometimes even a small change is enough to cause the hammer to miss the nail.

8

Building a strategy for Avon

The urge to diversify is a basic driving force inside Corporate America. In many ways, it is the dominant corporate strategy for a host of companies. Furthermore, the urge to diversify exists in all types of situations.

When things are going good, a company wants to branch out "to take advantage of the equity in our corporate or brand name."

When things are going bad, a company wants to branch out into other pastures where the grass is greener.

Both strategies are typical top-down moves. And both usually cause problems.

The "going good" strategy leads a company into what we call the line-extension trap.

The "going bad" strategy of diversifying into new fields can cause as many problems as line extension.

Avon is an example of the latter. Things were going bad in its basic business, so Avon went out and bought a couple of perfume companies.

When the going gets tough

Unfortunately, few top executives live by the maxim, "When the going gets tough, the tough get going."

They have their own version of this old maxim. It goes like this: "When the going gets tough, find someone else to go."

After a few handy folks have been sacrificed trying to turn things around, the next round of management tells the board that the market is flat. They can't expect a return to the glory days of yesteryear because the market has changed. The seeds are thus sown for a corporate move to the other side of the fence.

The next thing you read about are the new acquisitions. Management focuses on nearby markets where the grass is perceived to be a lot greener.

All this bodes badly for your basic business as other managers, sensing the loss of interest on the part of top management, begin to carefully review their personal agendas. No bold new moves are put forth and the company shifts into a "harvesting" mode, where it takes out a lot more than it puts in.

Sometimes you have to face the reality of a declining business. But unless your business is built on a fad, no business disappears overnight. Furthermore, you are leaping from the frying pan into the fire when you chase new markets that others already dominate. Better to spend that money on a serious upgrading of the basic business you dominate.

Changing your course can lead you to overlook opportunities right in your own backyard.

Avon calling

The story of Avon has some of this in it. Long the leader in door-to-door selling of cosmetics, Avon found that things started to get difficult as more and more of these types of products moved from the not so accessible department stores to the very accessible drug and retail chains.

On top of that, the woman of the house wasn't around during the day to answer that famous doorbell. ("Ding dong, Avon calling.")

Gradually, direct selling to Main Street, U.S.A. began to lose some of its glamour as the category flattened out and became "mature."

This was one of the reasons Avon began to look over the fence at flashy Fifth Avenue and what was going on in the highly profitable $2 billion retail market for upscale fragrances.

They couldn't resist what they saw. In short order they engineered a retail launch of Catherine Deneuve fragrance and the acquisition of Giorgio, Inc. A few months later, Avon acquired Parfumes Stern, the marketer of Perry Ellis for men and Oscar de la Renta, Ruffles, and Valentino fragrances for women.

The logic was flawless. Avon's move to designer fragrances to be marketed through department stores probably wasn't hard to sell in the boardroom. Fewer and fewer women are home; they're out working. And working women have more disposable income than ever.

And the grass is a lot greener. As James Preston, the head of Avon's Beauty Group was reported to have said, "Where else can you find pretax margins in the 13 to 16 percent range and return on equity in the high 20s?"

Let's say you were appointed the new manager of marketing at Avon. What would you do about it? Where would you put your emphasis?

Facing problems at home

Your challenges are formidable. First, Avon's new competitors—Estée Lauder and Calvin Klein—are old hands at this fashion-driven, trendy business. Second, designer fragrances have had flat sales in recent years. Third, the style of promotion and advertising in upscale designer brands is very different from Avon's usual efforts. Mystery and fantasy are at as high a pitch as is the spending.

Obviously, this difficult effort will have to capture a great deal of your attention if it is to succeed.

What happens to your basic business while all this is going on? It's a very important question since Avon's cosmetic business is the biggest portion of your business.

Avon has been losing ground in recent years. Its share of cosmetics has declined 33 percent. (From a 12 percent to an 8 percent share.)

Regardless of the opportunity the new perfume acquisitions represent, we think you will first want to turn your attention to your core business, the beauty products.

Where do you start? Where do you find a tactic that will drive the basic business?

What's an Avon?

Obviously, you start in the mind of the prospect. And you start by asking a basic question: "What's an Avon?"

Or more precisely, "Is Avon a product or is Avon a channel?" Avon is obviously both, but the principle of focus comes into play. "Is Avon identified more as a product or more as a channel?"

You might suspect that Avon's perceptions are still summed up by that famous expression: "Ding dong, Avon calling."

Because Avon has come to stand for so many different beauty and decorative products, you might feel that Avon is perceived more as a sales channel than as a manufacturing company. You're probably right.

Avon represents the opportunity to buy beauty products at home or at work.

Let's say Avon is a channel. Fortunately, that's also Avon's uniqueness.

You can buy many different brands of shampoo, but only one shampoo brand can be ordered in and delivered to your home: Avon.

If your perceptions are accurate, your tactic has to be built around advertising the Avon channel, not the Avon products.

Your advertising should make your channel more important. Once in the door, your Avon representatives can sell a number of different products. Hopefully, among them will be your biggest profit makers.

If Avon has a stodgy image or perception, it must be because of the Avon representatives. After all, they stand for the company. The key question is: How do you reposition your representatives? How do you enhance what they represent so as to offer prospects a reason to seek out the Avon channel?

Obviously, the more this is done, the better your chances of increasing the percentage of beauty products that your customers will buy from their Avon representatives.

A look at the competition

A tactic is a competitive mental angle. If Avon is a channel, what is Avon's competition? What other channels compete with Avon? There are two major competitors:

1. *The department store.* If price is no object, a woman can go to a department store, sit down with a manufacturer's representative, and discuss and select customized cosmetics.

2. *The drug/grocery store.* If price is an object, a woman can go to a mass distribution outlet and pick out what she wants. No service is offered.

The third channel is Avon. What you represent is convenience. A woman can call an Avon representative or go through an Avon catalog and pick out what she wants. Avon will deliver it.

From your declining market share, it would appear that the other two channels are winning the battle.

If Avon is to regain share, you will have to find a way to split the difference between the department store and the mass merchandisers. Your channel should

offer some of the beauty consulting that the department store offers but at prices considerably closer to
what the drug/grocery store offers.

Here are two suggestions which in reality are opposite sides of the same tactical coin.

The Avon PBR

This approach calls for making the Avon salesperson a
Personal Beauty Representative (PBR, for short) as opposed to a catalog distributor and order taker.

Obviously, training is a big factor as is advertising to
build awareness for this role. (This part is the strategy
that would drive the PBR tactic.)

Because of the multitude of product offerings and
colors, you might surmise that cosmetics cause a great
deal of confusion in the mind of the consumer. The
PBR concept could play against this problem.

The Avon BC

Related to the PBR is a new piece of technology that
could make the Avon salesperson a true Personal
Beauty Representative.

You might consider equipping your most productive representatives with Beauty Computers (BCs). Pro-
grammed for things like skin type and hair color, this
small computer could aid the PBR in selecting products
for the customer that ensure that "you never looked so
good."

In reality, the BC could be a computer terminal that
would be connected to mainframes or regional minicomputers via telephone lines.

In addition to aiding your representatives, the Avon Beauty Computer could become a powerful advertising idea to help sell the channel. (The advertising tactic should drive the business strategy.)

In essence, the Beauty Computer is what makes the Avon representative a Personal Beauty Consultant rather than a salesperson.

You might find that the Beauty Computer is already being worked on at Avon. This shouldn't surprise you because it is an obvious idea. It's more a question of corporate commitment to the concept.

In other words, building the tactic into a strategy would require substantial amounts of time and financial resources. This is the area where the concept is likely to run aground.

With your bottom-up thinking, you have just impaled Avon's top management on the horns of a dilemma. Having sold the board on a big investment in designer fragrances, you are now asking for another trip to the corporate safe for the funds to invest in new technology and training.

Someone on the board might ask how management expects to fund both activities with limited resources? Your new retail effort might come under serious question and cause some embarrassment.

If those fears run through the CEO's mind, you just might lose your newfound Avon marketing job.

9

Making the changes

Building a tactic into a strategy invariably means making changes. As in the Avon example, the changes you have to make are not in the marketplace. What you must change is the company or its products.

What's fixed and what's variable? The market is fixed because your marketing efforts cannot make much of a change in its structure or buying patterns. Nor can you substantially change the mind of the prospect.

But hope springs eternal in the marketing breast. Marketing people believe they can change human behavior with the tools of advertising. That's like trying to change the weather by leaving your doors open.

The advertising industry spends the equivalent of $500 million each year in contributed advertising time and space in the war against illicit drugs.

The opposition, the drug dealers and wholesalers, spend nothing, even though their resources are enormous.

Stopping drugs is a very difficult problem. The tactical concept we suggested in Chapter 6 cannot hope to do more than dampen the demand somewhat. Marketing muscle is no substitute for human wants and desires.

The consumption of alcohol used to be just as illegal in the United States as the consumption of crack. So who won the battle against alcohol? The government or the people?

You can't fight city hall. You can't fight the marketplace. The objective of your marketing programs should not be to change minds. The objective of your marketing programs should be to take "unfair" advantage of the ideas and concepts already lurking up there on top of those necks.

"Unfair" is another way of defining the "edge" contributed to the program by the marketing strategy. It's what the coach supplies to the football or baseball team.

Marketing people often resist changes dictated by outside events or conditions. They take to heart Shakespeare's advice, "This above all: to thine own self be true." They forget these words were said by Polonius and you know what happened to him. (He got stabbed by Hamlet through the arras.)

Trying to change the marketplace

Top-down strategic planning almost always introduces an element of necessary change in the marketplace. The plan fails because the change isn't possible.

Much the same occurs in warfare. Hitler's southern strategy on the Russian front in 1942 called for the capture of Stalingrad to open the way to the Russian oil fields in the Caucasus.

But Stalingrad couldn't be taken by Colonel-General Friedrich Paulus.

Many a top-down marketing plan meets the same fate as Paulus's Sixth Army on the Don River. The plan is unhinged by its inability to overcome a single element in the prospect's mind. Xerox's grand strategy to become a major force in computers broke its back on the strongly held perception that Xerox means copiers, not computers.

"We can change that perception," said the powers-that-be at Xerox.

No, you can't. Several billion dollars later, Xerox still means copiers. (On balance, it's a good thing for Xerox that it does.)

The essence of bottom-up marketing is to accept the fixed points that exist in the mind and to make the necessary changes inside the company.

Don't try to force your way into the mind. *Change* your way into the mind. In the classic words of the men's store manager, "Turn on the blue lights. The man wants a blue suit."

Don't try to convince him he would look better in a brown suit, even though that may be true.

In the bottom-up process, the variables are always inside the company. Nor are the required changes necessarily of earth-shaking importance. Sometimes it's just a matter of turning on the blue lights.

Changing the name

As time moves on, some names tend to get out of date. Take Western Union, for example. Founded in 1851, this is the company that introduced the telegram, which put the Pony Express out of business a decade later. This is also the company that is in the process of putting itself out of business because it refuses to make the fundamental changes needed.

One hundred years after Western Union's founding, the telegram was still the mainstay of its business. But times were changing and the company tried to stay current.

Western Union launched the first domestic communications satellite. It pioneered electronic mail with Mailgram and then with Easy Link, its computer communications service.

After millions of dollars were spent to launch all of its new electronic services, what was the public's perception of Western Union? Right, a boy on a bicycle delivering a telegram.

Nor did the telegram service itself receive high marks from the public. "We knew it was a phony telegram," said an article in a prominent newsweekly, "because it arrived on time and there were no typographical errors."

Turn on the blue lights. Western Union needs a new name.

Instead of changing the name, Western Union chose to fight the perception. They spent millions on corporate advertising plus the millions spent to introduce the new services.

Said the chairman in the spring of 1984: "Our new services—Easy Link, electronic mail, Worldwide Telex, Airfone, and cellular radio—place Western Union at the forefront of our industry. While we continue to manage the business we inherited from the past, we will also continue to promote a steady stream of new services."

The steady stream has been all to no avail as Western Union continues to sink slowly in the west. Keep tuned to *The Wall Street Journal* for more news on the saga of the company with a nineteenth-century name in the twentieth century.

Names get out of tune

Names need to be tuned into what's in the mind of the prospect. Like Western Union's name, they often get out of tune.

With the rise of the deadly AIDS virus, the sale of AYDS diet candy declined 50 percent. Solution: Change the name.

Allegheny Airlines was going nowhere until it changed its name to USAir. (It didn't help that passengers used to call the carrier "Agony Airlines.")

Alphonso D'Abruzzo couldn't get a job on television until he changed his name to Alan Alda.

Before Haloid introduced the plain-paper copier, it added Xerox to its name.

Ralph Lipshitz couldn't give you the shirt off his back until he changed his name to Ralph Lauren.

Horse mackerel wasn't moving off the docks until an enterprising Boston dealer decided to call it tuna fish instead.

A researcher put a Sanyo label on an RCA electronic device and asked 900 people to compare it to an identical device with the RCA label. Seventy-six percent said the Sanyo product was better.

Don't fight the mindset of the prospect. Turn on the name lights instead.

Sambo's restaurant chain tried to fight for its name.

Sambo's, at one time the largest U.S. coffeehouse chain with more than 1000 units in operation, ended up in bankruptcy. A racist or sexist name won't make it in the mind today. If you have one, change it.

If your name doesn't support the tactic that you are building into a strategy, change your name. This is one of the key elements of the strategic side of the bottom-up process.

Name changes are more common than you might think. In a recent year a record 1753 American corporations changed their names.

Changing the product or service

This is the most common change that needs to be made in running a tactic up the strategy flagpole.

Take the bank that discovers an interesting tactical opportunity in its car loan business. While its competitors take 48 hours to process a car loan, this bank does the job in 24 hours.

A car loan in half the time is not a bad tactic in the competitive banking field. But given the nature of the business, it wouldn't be an exclusive service for very long.

This is always the fate of a tactic. If it doesn't work, you lose. If it does work, you get copied.

The bank turned its 24-hour car loan tactic into a strategy. It changed all of its procedures to speed up the banking process. It pushed decision making down to the local level. (One of its lending teams can approve a $10 million commercial loan, and that team meets daily.)

Once these changes were in place, the bank launched a marketing program to position itself as "the fast-moving bank."

"Time is money," said one ad. "People shouldn't hold up banks and banks shouldn't hold up people either," said another.

By preempting the fast-moving concept, the bank also blocked competitors from copying the concept.

Competitors feel no qualms about copying a tactic. American introduced AAdvantage, the frequent flier program. But that didn't stop almost every other airline from introducing its own frequent flier plans.

Strategies are different. A good strategy is hard to copy. Would the folks at National Car Rental tell the world that they "try harder"?

Lack of product discipline causes many companies to miss an opportunity to turn a tactical "product" success into a long-term corporate strategy.

Sony, for example, pioneered the concept of miniaturization in the electronic field. "Tummy TV" said the famous Sony advertisement.

Sony had the potential to dominate the concept of "small" in electronics. Yet Sony plunged into big television sets, including 48-inch projection equipment. (Volkswagen made much the same mistake.)

The discipline to restrict new product introductions to a narrow strategic field is sadly lacking among most corporate managers. They want it all. "We own small. Now let's go out and own big, too," is the typical scenario of a company which winds up owning nothing.

Changing the price

We should have said "setting the price right in the first place." After the psychological price of a product has been established, it's difficult to change it.

Cadillac can't sell $56,000 Allantés because in the mind a Cadillac isn't a $56,000 product.

Absolut sells vodka for $12 a fifth because of the higher price, not in spite of it. High price is absolutely necessary to position the product as a superpremium vodka.

Another product that was priced right is Bally shoes. Bally is a big seller of shoes at the high end of the American market.

If you visit Switzerland, Bally's home base, you find some interesting facts. Bally isn't a high-priced shoe. Bally isn't a low-priced shoe.

Bally makes shoes for all price points. By selecting a high-end tactic, Bally was able to develop an effective strategy for the American market.

An even stranger situation is represented by Beefeater gin. In the United Kingdom, its country of origin, Beefeater is a low-priced product. In the United States, there was no room in the mind for another low-priced gin.

So, in America, Beefeater became a high-priced gin. It's become a very successful high-priced gin with almost a million cases sold every year.

Changing the mind

A mind is the most difficult thing in the world to change. It involves "forgetting" one set of perceptions and "remembering" another.

Did you ever try to forget something?

What's the most embarrassing moment in your life? Did someone ever say something to you that hurt you deeply?

Now try to forget that moment. You can't. That's the essence of the mind-changing problem.

Furthermore, the process of trying to change a mind often has the opposite effect. It tends to reinforce a previously held opinion.

When Richard Nixon said, "I will not resign," the public thought otherwise. (Anyone who says he will not resign four times, as Nixon did, will obviously someday resign.)

If someone says to you, "I'm honest," you think the opposite. (He must think I think he's dishonest. Otherwise, why did he say that?)

We call this phenomenon "the implication of the opposite." What you say implies the opposite of what you say.

If you return home from a business trip and tell your spouse you didn't get drunk and you didn't fool around, what do you suppose your husband or wife is going to think?

How did the folks at Exxon try to convince prospects they weren't going to fold their office systems line? They ran an advertising program declaring their "commitment" to the market.

"Remember," said the ads, "when you buy Exxon equipment, you buy our commitment to your future."

What the reader thought was, "They must think I think they're going to go out of business." Which, of course, they did.

IBM doesn't run advertisements announcing its commitment to office automation. If it did, customers would start to worry.

You should put your marketing messages under the implication microscope. Reverse the message and see if that is really what you want to imply.

Since every statement you make implies the opposite, stridency seldom works. It's too easy for the reader or viewer to reverse the message.

When a car dealer screams, "We're selling cars like crazy," the prospect says to himself, "They must think I don't think they're selling a lot of cars."

If stridency doesn't work in advertising or marketing, what does?

Finding a competitive mental angle that already exists in the mind. (It may even be a negative one.) That's your advertising tactic that will work.

Don't try to change minds.

10

Shifting the battlefield

If you're not winning the battle, shift the battlefield. This maxim of war works on marketing as well as on military battlefields.

Things were not going well for General Douglas MacArthur's Pacific campaign in the early days of World War II.

He lost Bataan, Corregidor, and the Phillippines. He lost eight capital ships at Pearl Harbor. Guam and Wake Island fell and he almost lost Midway. An invasion of Australia was threatened.

Instead of meeting the Japanese head to head, MacArthur shifted his forces to an "island-hopping" campaign and turned the tide of battle in the Pacific.

MacArthur did the same thing in the Korean war. Instead of pushing out from Pusan, he launched a flanking attack at Inchon and quickly knocked the

North Koreans all the way to China. (He may have
overdone things.)

While often used in the military, shifting the battlefield is a tactic that corporate generals seem to be un-
comfortable with.

On business battlefields, head honchos would rather
hang in there and slug it out. They believe in an "all we
need is a better effort" strategy.

Better products, better advertising, better sales
training, better pricing, to name a few of the more popular "betters."

Endless amounts of corporate time and effort go into
meetings aimed at making things better. Yet market share
often fails to improve and things don't get any better.

Face reality. Many times you have to recognize the
fact that the battle cannot be won and the chances for
victory are beginning to swing toward the enemy.

"A penetrating eye," says Clausewitz, "is a more necessary and useful quality for a general than craftiness."

Even if the battle is a stalemate, a military general
hates to be caught in costly trench warfare where casualties continue to mount and gains are hard to come by.
That is why generals are usually quick to maneuver in
an effort to shift things in their favor.

Beating a dead horse

Quite the opposite happens in business. Management
continues to send troops charging up the same hill.
They might complain about the lack of progress, but
rarely do they want to admit defeat.

A "can do" attitude gets high marks in the corporation, while "defeatists" are tagged as poor team players
and given low marks.

One of us had a personal experience that illustrates
the attitude. At the time, he was involved with the marketing of Uniroyal tires.

At a big management meeting, he suggested that
winning the tire war against the likes of Goodyear,
Firestone, Goodrich, and Michelin was highly unlikely.

Since Uniroyal was losing money in passenger
tires, perhaps a shift in focus toward truck tires was
called for since they were a lot more profitable. This
suggestion was met with a room full of cold stares
and a bare acknowledgment of the suggestion. It was
back to the battle.

(History has shown that a shift toward truck tires
would not have been a bad idea for Uniroyal because
passenger tire losses mounted, eventually forcing the
company to merge itself out of existence.)

What makes management so reluctant to shift the
battlefield is the fact that change is required. People are
rarely comfortable with change.

This reluctance is probably based on the old maxim
that a bird in the hand is worth two in the bush. Unfortunately, that old saw never dealt with the fact that
someone is out there taking those birds out of your
hands. So you're better off getting into the bushes as
soon as possible to find those two unclaimed birds.

Not all managers are reluctant to change. There appear to be at least four types of successful tactical
shifts.

Shifting the audience

Cigarette brands used to be unisex brands, appealing to men and women alike. Then Philip Morris launched Marlboro as a woman's brand of cigarette.

As a woman's brand, Marlboro went nowhere. But rather than continue a losing battle, Philip Morris brought in the cowboy and shifted the focus to men. Today Marlboro is the No. 1 cigarette in the world.

Years later Philip Morris tried the woman's market again. The brand was called Virginia Slims, which quickly became a big success. Sometimes it's just a question of timing.

What works in cigarettes also works in cars. Once upon a time, Pontiac was a conservative family car for older people. Pontiac competed with other conservative cars like DeSoto, Oldsmobile, Buick, and Mercury.

In the sixties Pontiac was headed up by John DeLorean. It was DeLorean's brilliant idea to shift the Pontiac audience focus from family to youth. The GTO and the LeMans were born, and Pontiac started down the hot car road.

Today Pontiac still "builds excitement" for the younger automobile buyer. Over the years Pontiac has been GM's most successful division.

More than the younger set buy Pontiacs. The shift has also attracted older buyers who want to think and act young.

What works in cars also works in colas. Another successful shift to the younger set was Pepsi-Cola's move to preempt the Pepsi Generation. Leaving the old folks to shift for themselves, Pepsi dazzled the kids with Michael Jackson, Don Johnson, and Lionel Ritchie.

The Pepsi-Cola program was based on the observation that teenagers want their own thing. They don't want your thing.

If you have a teenager at home, you can prove it to yourself. The next time the kid brings home some records, just pick up one at random and say, "I love their music. That's my favorite group."

That kid will never play that record again.

More than kids, of course, became Pepsi drinkers. The Pepsi Generation appeals to kids of all ages. Fifty-five-year-old folks who want to think they're 48 drink Pepsi.

It was the success of this shift that eventually led Coca-Cola to unfurl New Coke, a sweeter product it hoped would put a dent in the Pepsi Generation. (All it did was put a dent in Coca-Cola's reputation.)

This is a good example of the secondary benefits of a tactical shift. In both war and business, when a successful shift is executed, the competition is forced to react.

Sometimes competition reacts badly and weakens what was once a strong position. This presents new opportunities to exploit.

One of the ways to find a tactic is by analogy. That is, a tactic that works in one situation is likely to work in another.

The Pepsi-Cola pattern, for example, can be applied to Burger King.

Like Pepsi, Burger King is No. 2 to an institution. McDonald's is a powerful marketing machine with an emotional lock on its market. McDonald's has moved into the mental category reserved for institutions like motherhood, night baseball, and apple pie.

Burger King used to emulate its major competitor. Remember the magical Burger King? Most people have forgotten this royal knockoff of Ronald McDonald.

In the early eighties, Burger King shifted the battlefield. Instead of trying to outdo McDonald's, it tried to *undo* McDonald's with a program called "broiling, not frying."

While "broiling, not frying" is an effective tactic, it's not a great strategy. It hasn't been carried to the emotional level, which only a great strategy can sustain. It needs to be hammered in.

In some ways the flame-broiling idea is like the Pepsi Challenge. Both are tactical points of difference.

In Pepsi's case, the sweeter taste appealed to teenagers, the core market for cola drinks. The Pepsi Generation is the strategic, emotional elevation of the "sweeter product" tactic.

The same idea, in reverse, can work for Burger King. What's the burger analogy for the older kid who drinks Coca-Cola?

It's the younger kid who is in love with McDonald's. Go down to the front and look around. Those swings and slides and Ronald McDonalds have an enormous appeal to the kindergarten crowd.

This observation sets up an opportunity for an audience shift for Burger King. But instead of using the Pepsi approach of appealing to the younger kid, the obvious Burger King strategy is to appeal to the older kid.

"Grow up to Burger King" is the strategic development of the flame-broiling tactic.

To turn the flame-broiling tactic into a grow-up strategy, Burger King would have to make some changes. They'd have to get rid of the swings and slides that some of their units have. They'd also have to drop the kiddie meals on the menu.

One powerful way to execute the "grow-up" strategy is an approach called "rite of passage."

In Burger King's case, a rite of passage could be the moment in time when a kid is no longer a kid.

For example, on the first day of high school a freshman runs into upperclassmen who offer to buy him a burger.

"At McDonald's?" asks the kid.

"You're not in grade school anymore," says one of the older kids.

"That's Kiddieland," scoffs a second kid. "We're taking you to Burger King."

Wouldn't a narrow approach like this sacrifice a lot of business? After all, a fast-food hamburger restaurant serves a broad spectrum of customers from kids to grownups.

The target is not the market

Some of the most dramatic marketing victories have been won by recognizing a simple fact: the tactical target of your communications program does not have to be the same as the market.

An obvious example of this principle is the advertising for Marlboro cigarettes. If you were a recent arrival from Mars, you would think that America is populated by cowboys. Either that or cowboys smoke a lot of cigarettes.

In spite of the fact that the ads show only cowboys smoking the brand, Marlboro has become the No. 1

brand of cigarette, among women as well as men. The tactical target is not the strategic market.

Prospects don't take your advertising personally. Rather, they extract from the message ideas and concepts that they can utilize in their own lives. Those ideas might be in direct conflict with the "obvious" message of the advertisement.

Smoking is a masculine activity, among women as well as men. People smoke cigarettes to enhance their masculinity.

What better symbol of masculinity than the cowboy? It's a boy's dream of heaven, week after week without shaving or showering.

(Whatever the views of the majority, there is always room for the opposite tactic. Witness the success of Virginia Slims.)

Marketing managers who accept the power of symbolism in tobacco and liquor will often reject it in their own products, which they believe are too serious for a symbolic approach.

Not true. Very few products should be targeted at the total market. Most programs would benefit from the emotional opportunities created by a narrowing of the target audience. Again, it's the power of focus.

Pepsi's tactic in the cola war illustrates the advantages of targeting the core rather than the whole market.

Coke's strength is its heritage. Only seven people in the history of the world have known Coca-Cola's formula, which remains locked in the vault of the Trust Company of Georgia.

Coke's 100-year-old heritage also means that the older you are, the more likely you are to drink Coca-

Cola. The younger you are, the more likely you are to drink Pepsi-Cola.

Narrowing the target to a portion of the market allows Pepsi to exploit sibling rivalry. If the older sibling drinks Coke, the younger sibling wants to drink something different.

The Pepsi Generation also has the advantage of targeting the core of the market. Teenagers drink more soft drinks than any other age group. In one sense, colas are a teenage product.

After all that effort, who drinks Pepsi-Cola? Everybody does. That is, all age groups purchase substantial quantities of Pepsi.

You may have read stories in the press about the "comeback at Coke." Yet the numbers tell the real story. Currently Coca-Cola outsells Pepsi-Cola in the United States about 10 to 9.

In theory, the leader should outsell No. 2 by two to one. Keeping the battle close is a tremendous moral victory for Pepsi.

The same principle applies to Burger King. A teenage target is not going to kill the market. Burgers are a teenage product ... for kids of any age. Burger King is a hamburger joint that appeals to sophisticated teenagers ... of any age.

There are many other products where the target is designed to be considerably different from the market.

Seventeen magazine has a name and editorial position targeted specifically at 17-year-old girls.

But who reads *Seventeen*? Girls who are 13, 14, 15, and 16 years old, that's who. When a young woman grows up to be 17, she usually outgrows *Seventeen* magazine.

What's the market for ID cards? People who are 18, 19, and 20 years old, that's who. When a person gets to be 21, there's no need for an ID card.

Virginia Slims is a cigarette whose target is liberated women and female swingers. Each ad shows a woman who is 25 and "with it." But the market is the middle-aged woman who aspires to that lifestyle. The average Virginia Slims smoker is more like 45.

Both Virginia Slims and *Seventeen* appeal to aspirations and not reality.

The Corvette is a car that has a strong position with teenage boys and a market of golden oldies. (Even if the teenager got one free, he couldn't afford the insurance to drive it.)

Johnson's Baby Shampoo has a healthy share of the adult market. Would the company be better off calling the product "Johnson's Everybody Shampoo"?

Of course not. Adults use Johnson's because it *is* a baby shampoo. Yet this message is lost on many marketing people who try to appeal to everybody.

Who wants to buy a product that everybody buys? Nobody.

Shifting the product

Sometimes you have to realize that you have the wrong product in a category.

In the radio station wars, for example, if you're the third "soft rock" entry in a market, you're stuck in the trenches with few options. Your best chance probably lies in looking around for a new format with less competition. Then you find a new set of call letters and shift the battlefield with a new product.

This was exactly the case recently in New York's radio wars. NBC's soft-rock station WYNY-FM made its reputation in the early eighties with a musical format that appealed to adults. Its share grew to a five rating, which was enough to put the station in second place in the competitive New York market. Profits were $6 million a year.

But then the enemy struck. A top 40 station, Z-100, picked off the younger end of WYNY's audience. The older end went to WLTW-FM, a "light music" station.

Unfortunately, WYNY fought the battle too long. In short order it was losing $2.5 million a year.

Recently WYNY shifted the battlefield. It switched from soft rock to country music since there were no country stations in New York at the time. In short order its ratings jumped more than a share point. There are signs of a turnaround.

Another successful "product shift" took place in the highly competitive movie industry.

Walt Disney is king of the "G" movies (for general audiences). Unfortunately, in this wide-open, sexually liberated world, no one other than tiny tots wants to see a G movie anymore. PG or R movies are where the big bucks are.

So Disney Studios ventured into the adult movie world with some properties they called Disney films, even though they were a long way from being in the Mickey Mouse mold.

They bombed.

What the studio quickly discovered was that the Disney name turned off teenagers and grown-ups looking for something a little more risqué than what Uncle Walt was known for.

Then Ronald L. Miller, Walt Disney's son-in-law, came up with a "product shift" strategy. He created an adult label called Touchstone Pictures.

Thanks to movies like *Down and Out in Beverly Hills, Three Men and a Baby,* and *Who Framed Roger Rabbit?,* Touchstone has become a very successful producer of motion pictures.

The company now has two powerful entities: the Disney name and product for the family business and the Touchstone name for the adult business.

So far, everyone is living happily ever after.

Shifting the focus

Many times you have to tighten things up in order to find success. In other words, you must narrow your efforts by sacrificing some of your business.

Shifting the focus means moving from being a generalist to becoming a specialist. If things work out, you build an even bigger business. Shifting the focus could also be called the "less is more" approach to marketing.

Long ago and far away, a small regional furniture retailer had a problem. Its name was Love Furniture Store. (No, it didn't sell water beds.) Love Furniture Store sold a full line of medium-priced furniture such as chairs, sofas, end tables, coffee tables, and such.

But the furniture world was changing. The big discount operators such as Levitz were entering the market. Love Furniture knew that a full-line, immediate-delivery discount operator like Levitz would be tough to beat.

So Love decided to reduce its focus. But what could it sacrifice?

Love decided to eliminate case goods: dressers, cabinets, wall units. (These products had a bad track record for long delivery times.)

It focused on chairs and upholstered products. Without the case goods, Love could offer shorter delivery times.

But a narrow focus doesn't work without a narrow focus name. The obvious answer to the name question: "Sofas and Chairs."

Love christened a store with the new name and recorded the most successful opening it ever had.

On a grander scale, this type of focus shift was illustrated by the story of Interstate Department Stores. (You'll recognize the company by its new name, Toys "Я" Us.)

That's right. Once upon a time, this immensely successful retailer was struggling along in the discount department store wars. Interstate was stuck with chains like Topps and others that were failing.

Then it bought Toys "Я" Us in an embryonic state, went into bankruptcy, and emerged as strictly a toy retailer.

The rest is history.

How historic? Well, Toys "Я" Us now has 350 stores which control more than 20 percent of the $13 billion toy market. In this case, less is a lot more.

Shifting the distribution

An interesting battlefield shift can be prompted by running out of room in your traditional channel of distribution. In other words, you try to increase sales by adding a new channel of distribution.

A successful example of a tactical distribution shift can be found in pantyhose.

For years Hanes was the main pantyhose player in the department store channel. But as the category grew, it found itself competing with lower-priced brands or the store's house brand.

Does it drop the price of Hanes, thus undercutting its high-quality perception? Or does it introduce a low-priced brand of its own?

Maybe neither. Recognizing the difficulty of winning the price wars, Hanes developed a distribution shift.

Hanes opened up a second front in the grocery store channel, a place where pantyhose had never been sold before. Just as important, it gave the new pantyhose product a name that sounded like it belonged in a grocery store.

The new product was called L'eggs. Hanes delivered and stocked L'eggs in the same way that real eggs are delivered and stocked.

This classic distribution shift built a large and very successful brand of pantyhose.

A similar grocery store success can be found at the checkout counter. You can't pay for your groceries without passing the *National Enquirer* and its numerous sidekicks.

Famous for those eye-catching headlines, the paper shifted distribution from the newsstand to the grocery store. Those headlines just wouldn't be as visible surrounded by a sea of other newspapers and magazines.

You see the same tactical shifts in office supplies. A number of large discount operators such as Quill and

Reliable are selling to the small business and home office markets via direct mail catalog instead of through dealers.

The direct marketers' share of the office supply industry is over 10 percent and climbing.

There are many ways to shift the battlefield. The options are limited only by your creativity and your willingness to look for them out in the marketplace rather than inside your own organization.

11

Shifting the battlefield at GM

To better understand the methodology behind the "shifting the battlefield" tactic, it might be of interest to apply the principles to a current battle.

In other words, let's play general and try to figure out what kind of shift should be considered in a losing battle. Take the problems of General Motors trying to do battle with BMW, Mercedes-Benz, and other imports at the high end.

This part of the market has not produced many victories for General Motors. In fact, it has been somewhat of an embarrassment. The latest example is the Allanté, named by *Automotive News* as the "flop of the year."

The Allanté wasn't GM's first move against the high-end market.

Introducing the Seville

GM's first move was to send its crack Cadillac division out to do battle with those upstarts from Germany. Obviously, much of this activity was at the behest of Cadillac dealers who were watching some of their long-term customers move up to Mercedes.

Since the German luxury vehicles are smaller than a Cadillac, GM attacked with a smaller, newly designed model called the Seville. Initially the Seville didn't take many German prisoners.

The problem was simple. Who ever heard of a small Cadillac? It wasn't until they made the Seville as big as a Cadillac that it became a big success. But instead of taking business away from BMW or Mercedes, the Seville took business away from Fleetwoods and Broughams.

Introducing the Cimarron

Once the Seville became a big car, GM's next move was to send another small, newly designed model into battle. It was called the Cadillac Cimarron and it was a big bomb. It took business from no one.

After meeting with 20 Cadillac dealers, Ross Perot was quoted in *Fortune* magazine as saying, "A Cadillac needs to look different from a Chevrolet or it's kind of tough to sell." It was back to the drawing boards.

Introducing the Allanté

Undaunted, GM decided on yet another small Cadillac. But since big Mercedes and BMWs were now going for $50,000 and up, GM decided to go "first cabin."

Everyone boarded a plane for Italy, and there the Cadillac Allanté was born. This would do the trick. It was small and European-designed, and it cost $56,000. What more could a Mercedes prospect want? It was the ultimate weapon in the automotive wars.

So far the Allanté has turned out to be another bomb like the Cimarron. Unless sales pick up, it will go off in GM's face with little damage to Mercedes and BMW and Jaguar.

Introducing reality

What's to be done? Well, first GM has to recognize that the Cadillac division can't win the battle against the expensive imports. (Facing reality, we call it.)

The perception of a Cadillac in the mind of the auto buyer is a strong one. A Cadillac is a big, moderately expensive car with little prestige in this era of $70,000 BMWs. If I spend $56,000 for an Allanté, I don't want to have my neighbors think I own a $25,000 car.

The Cadillac division should be sent back to fighting Lincoln-Mercury. This Ford division has made some gains at Cadillac's expense. As Cadillac made its cars smaller, less distinctive, and more like a Mercedes, car buyers started to turn to the big Lincoln Town Cars.

Reintroducing the LaSalle

We would develop a "product shift" tactic. In other words, what's needed is a new GM brand in the superpremium segment of the market. As it happens, GM already owns the perfect name.

We would encourage GM to bring back the LaSalle. (For our younger readers, the LaSalle was one of the great classic cars of the twenties and thirties. Although part of the Cadillac family, LaSalle was usually treated as a separate brand.)

The irony of bringing back the LaSalle brand to compete with the European cars is the fact that it was originally conceived as a car with a "European look." It was modeled after the French Hispano-Suiza, a car only the historians remember.

Today's version would obviously have to be smaller and quite expensive like the European sedans. And most important, it would have to be sold by a new breed of LaSalle dealers. Not Cadillac dealers. (In the same way that Acuras are sold by Acura dealers, not Honda dealers.)

While this kind of tactic shift might have worked better years ago, it still is the only move GM can make today if it wants a larger share of the superpremium segment.

At those prices, who wouldn't want a larger piece?

12

Testing your strategy

To win a marketing war, you have to win the battle at the tactical level. You have to win the battle in the mind of the prospect.

If the mind is the battleground, then it should come as no surprise that advertising is the key tactical weapon in a marketing war.

Like an artillery shell, an advertisement or a commercial has the ability to make an impact on a broad segment of the market. With advertising you can literally create customers wholesale if, of course, you are properly zeroed in on your target.

Most companies know this. Which is why the volume of advertising is reaching astronomical proportions. As the volume increases, the relative effectiveness decreases. With the customer hunkered down in his or her mental foxhole, it becomes harder and harder to score a hit in our overcommunicated society.

Testing your advertising

With volume up and effectiveness down, advertising has become the focus of intensive research. Companies want to know in advance if their proposed advertising will work or not. That's why advertising research is also reaching astronomical proportions.

But advertising research has severe limitations. When Doyle Dane Bernbach tested the first batch of "Avis is only No. 2" advertisements, results were dismal.

Car rental customers hated the prototype ads. The client didn't like them. Bill Bernbach didn't like them.

But Robert Townsend, the new chairman of Avis, had promised his new agency that he would run the ads without change if only Doyle Dane would take his account.

So the ads ran and were an instant success. Even today, people remember the slogan, "Avis is only No. 2 in rent-a-cars. So why go with us? We try harder."

Hertz's 56 percent market share soon fell a full 6 points, while Avis's share rose by the same amount. That's a 12 percent shift that took place almost overnight. Furthermore, Avis started to make money after 13 straight years of red ink.

You can't test an individual ad or a marketing tactic. Like the Avis example, the results of an advertising test don't mean much of anything because the test is artificial.

The only test that reproduces reality is a test that exposes the prospect to the full weight of the strategy.

In the case of Avis, you'd have to find a way to expose the prospect to what the press was going to say about the advertising, to what Hertz was going to say (or not say), and especially to the smiling faces and the

"We try harder" buttons on the Avis personnel behind the counter.

That's impossible without running the program. So the best you can do to test your strategy is to try to present to prospects a total picture of what is going to happen.

Don't show prospects an ad and ask for their comments. They instantly turn into advertising experts.

Your prospects-turned-advertising-experts will be quick to give you their advice on layout, typography, photography, headlines. Everyone likes to play the role of advertising expert. Not only that, the confidence level of prospects is extremely high. They are certain they know for sure what will sell them and what won't sell them.

Consider the facts. Most major advertising programs that run are tested. They don't run if they don't test exceptionally well.

Yet most advertising is ineffective. Mathematically, that has to be true. In a given market four or five brands will develop marketing programs designed to increase market share. Yet on average, no one will increase market share, which in total remains at 100 percent. (In its purest form marketing, like war, is a zero-sum game.)

For one brand to increase market share, there has to be at least one loser. (Avis's increase came at the expense of Hertz.)

Given the mental and mathematical obstacles to marketing success, you should be extremely leery of all consumer testing.

The paradox is that the more novel and unique the program, the more likely it will succeed and the less likely it will test well. (Imagine a market test of Jackson Pollock's first painting or Bruce Springsteen's first record.)

Checking out the prospect

Despite our advice, before you spend your millions you'll want to check out the prospect. Here are some suggestions on what to look for.

Forget the numbers in the research report. These represent artificial responses to artificial questions asked in an artificial atmosphere.

Question: Would you spend $150 an ounce for a perfume called Obsession? (Translation: Are you stupid?)

Answer: No. (Translation: I'm not stupid.)

Obsession, of course, is a big winner in the perfume wars.

Then there's the constant pressure to extend the line. What keeps line extension alive in the hearts and minds of Corporate America is the fact that it tests well.

Put yourself in front of the one-way mirror and answer this question: "Which one of these two popcorns would you buy? Pillsbury microwave popcorn or Pop Secret microwave popcorn?"

Before Pop Secret was introduced you never heard of it, so naturally your answer is "Pillsbury."

Pillsbury popcorn died in the microwave oven, and Pop Secret is a big success, second only to Orville.

What kills line extension in the marketplace is the confusion factor. (Pillsbury means dough, not popcorn.) What keeps line extension alive in the focus group is the prospect's perfectionism. No one wants to admit that he or she could possibly confuse popcorn with the Doughboy.

Picking the interesting tactic

What's the secret of evaluating a focus group or customer research of any kind?

First of all, you have to make sure your tactical concept is "interesting." It's better to be interesting but hated than it is to be liked but dull.

Pillsbury is a dull, inappropriate name for a popcorn. Pop Secret, at least, suggests that there might be a secret of some kind in the formula or packaging. "That's interesting."

The definition of interesting is the same as the definition of "news." To be interesting, a concept must be "different." "Man bites dog," for example.

What happens when people are exposed to a concept that is different? They find it interesting, but they also reject it. It's human nature to be fascinated by but to reject anything that is different.

I might read the *National Enquirer,* but I don't want to be 8 feet tall, weigh 800 pounds, or have 42 kids, to summarize three recent stories.

Advertising agencies are well aware of the need to break through the media clutter by being interesting. Unfortunately, they often solve the creative problem by putting the differences into the irrelevant elements rather than into the tactical concept itself.

Normally they can't change the strategy since it has been dictated to them by the client in the typical top-down mode of operation.

That's why you'll see such absurdities on television as Joe Isuzu. The world's champion liar, Joe has driven his Isuzu to the top of Mount Everest. His secret? He used snow tires.

Do consumers relate to such nonsense? Sure, they remember the nonsense and forget the sense.

When someone says, "I saw this terrific commercial on TV last night," you know what's coming. The next words out of the mouth usually are, "I forgot the name of the product, but let me tell you about the commercial."

No wonder people remember Joe the liar but don't remember why they should buy one of his cars. In spite of spending $30 million a year on advertising, Isuzu manages to sell fewer than 40,000 cars a year in the U.S. market.

Compare that with Honda and Toyota, each of which sells more than 600,000 cars a year in the U.S. market.

Hyundai sells more than 250,000 cars a year.

Even Audi and Yugo manage to outsell Joe Isuzu.

So what was the most admired, most awarded, most respected advertising campaign in recent years? The Joe Isuzu campaign, and that's no lie.

How do you make your strategy interesting? That, of course, is a top-down way of thinking. In the bottom-up mode, you don't try to make your strategy interesting.

You pick an interesting tactic in the first place.

"Two pizzas for the price of one." That's interesting.

"When it absolutely, positively has to be there overnight." That's interesting.

"Grow up, kid, to flame-broiling." That's interesting.

The interest, of course, has to be germane to the product or service. And since advertising is the key tactical weapon in a marketing war, the idea has to be an interesting advertising idea.

That's why the advertising tactic should dictate business strategy.

Checking out the sales force

A good idea should be easy to sell to the sales force, right?

Wrong. A good idea is very difficult to sell to the sales force. They are too close to the situation. They know too much. They're as expert as the prospect.

A tactical idea that is simple enough to cut through the clutter to make an impact on the prospect is too simple for the sales force.

Should you sidestep the sales force and concentrate on the prospect? You do so at your own peril.

If your sales force isn't enthusiastically behind your program, it isn't going to work, no matter how brilliant it is.

So testing your program with the sales force involves selling them, not seeking out their opinions. If you can't sell it to them, you're in trouble.

Put everything into your sales pitch, including your own enthusiasm. Sales people love a good sales presentation.

If you can sell them, they in turn will sell the distributor or the ultimate customer. But it's a real challenge.

Checking out the press

It's difficult to get Dan Rather on the phone to ask him if he likes the strategy behind your new marketing program.

You have to do it indirectly. The key question to ask yourself: "Does the concept have news value?"

Maybe it will never make the 7 o'clock news, or even page 7 of your weekly newspaper. No matter, the concepts that work best "feel" like news.

When Pepsi-Cola launched Slice, the first carbonated beverage with 10 percent fruit juice, the introduction made news across the country.

When IBM launched an advertising program that positioned the company as "the bigger picture," every major U.S. publication ignored the introduction.

The bigger picture? IBM is a $54 billion company. Big Blue is already bigger than all of its competitors put together. Where's the news value in being a bigger picture?

When Avis launched the "Avis is No. 2" concept, it generated a rash of human interest stories in the press. Even the Vice President of the United States joked about having to try harder because "I'm only No. 2."

Checking out the competition

It's probably easier to get a reaction from Dan Rather or Tom Brokaw than it is to get your competition to evaluate your program in advance.

In the best of all possible worlds, you could show the program to each of your major competitors. If each one says "I hate it," you know you have a potential winner.

That's a highly unlikely scenario. But there is a way to accomplish much the same thing. It's called a logic check.

To check the logic of your proposition, you reverse the statement to see if the reversal is appropriate for your major competitor.

Avis is only No. 2 in rent-a-cars, so we have to try harder. What would the opposite of this statement be?

Hertz is No. 1 in rent-a-cars, so we can rest on our laurels. We don't have to try very hard. That's perfect, from the point of view of Avis. That will drive business from Hertz to Avis. If the prospect even imagines the representative behind the Hertz counter thinking like that, he or she will make the move.

Something special in the air. That's the slogan of American Airlines, the No. 2 airline. Let's reverse it for No. 1.

Something unspecial in the air. United is unspecial? United is the airline that widely advertises that it flies to Hawaii, among other special places.

Something special in the air doesn't get off the ground for American. Did you even know that was American's slogan? Probably not. It doesn't fit American's competitive situation.

Checking out the product line

One of the most dangerous aspects of the "strategy-first crowd" is the notion that a line extension can lead an independent life of its own.

Top-down organizations will take a line-extended brand and give it a separate marketing department, a separate sales force, a separate advertising budget.

Diet Coke has all of these things, including a separate

advertising agency. But the soft drinker takes one look at Diet Coke and thinks "Regular Coke without the calories."

All that separation does is to confuse the folks at Coca-Cola into thinking they have two brands when all they have is two flavors.

Test everything that has the same name on it because everything with the same name on it is locked together in the mind of the prospect.

The success of Diet Coke has come at the expense of regular Coke. That might be hard to see because there has been an explosion in sales of diet soft drinks generally. (As long as NutraSweet is cheaper than high-fructose corn syrup, Coca-Cola shouldn't care which product the customer drinks.)

Miller High Life, Miller Lite, and Miller Genuine Draft are three flavors of the same brand. When one goes up, the other two go down.

Coors Light follows the same pattern. It's going up as the regular goes down, illustrating the connectivity concept. The Silver Bullet used in the Coors Light commercials has found its target: Coors Regular.

The last brand to jump into the "light" pool was Budweiser. Anheuser-Busch is in the process of making Bud Light the No. 1 yuppie beer. Spokesdog Spuds MacKenzie and his three beautiful Spudettes are making Bud Light everything that Budweiser isn't.

Does Anheuser-Busch really think that Joe Sixpack doesn't watch these shenanigans? Well he does. Sooner or later Budweiser is going to start down the same road as Miller and Coors.

When two brands have the same name, they are locked together in the mind. You have to test both.

Spuds MacKenzie might be a barn burner for Bud

Light. The question is, What is that bull terrier going to do to the Budweiser name in the long run?

If the boys in the BMWs are drinking Bud Light, will the fellows in the Ford Broncos continue to drink Budweiser?

13

Selling your strategy

Now's the time to gather up what you've learned when you've tested your strategy and package it for an internal sell.

Presumably, you will need to go all the way to the CEO. You may get more attention to your ideas than you might think.

Now that the stock market has died down, management ought to be ready to get back to basics.

Until Black Monday, most companies could make more money buying and selling stock or buying and selling companies than they could in selling products. No longer.

Instead of promoting the company's stock, top management should start thinking about promoting the company's products.

Maybe what's bad for the market is good for marketing. Maybe management now has the time to listen to the big marketing concept that will blow away the competition.

Let's say you've found that perfect point of attack, the single, highly focused tactic that you've meticulously built into a powerful strategy.

Now you're in the boardroom making the presentation to top management. Your biggest problem is complacency. Your biggest problem is not getting a yes or a no. Your biggest problem is getting a yawn.

The trainee and the veteran

A young General Electric trainee was trying to sell a marketing program to the crusty veteran in charge of small electric motors. The trainee had assembled his thoughts in a desktop flip chart and was bravely going through it. As the presentation headed for the close, the trainee noticed that the marketing manager had lost interest and was looking out the window. The young man became nervous.

The veteran, noticing the trainee's problem, turned to him and said, "Put that flip chart down, kid, and I'll tell you some of the facts of life at General Electric."

"Look, we're talking about GE motors. The problem isn't out there in the market. The problem is in here. Show me a flip chart that gets every son-of-a-bitch in the building pointed in the same direction and we can level anything out there."

That wasn't exactly bottom-up thinking, but the guy had a point. It's not enough to find that brilliant tactic which you've turned into a powerful strategy. You also have to turn your own company on if your program is to work.

You have to get everyone excited and enthusiastic. You have to get everyone in the building pointed in the same direction.

Keep it simple

Don't try to sell your program "by the numbers." One of the worst things that has ever happened to marketing people is the invention of the spread sheet. Lotus 1-2-3 has created more dull presentations than any single business development since the overhead projector.

Act like a car salesperson. Don't trot out all the specifications and options.

Keep it simple. Fortunately, if you build your program from the bottom up, from a single tactic to a grand strategy, it will be simple. What you will be presenting is the single bold stroke that is not only dramatic, but effective too.

Present no alternatives

One of the most persistent questions you are likely to get from an internal audience has to do with alternatives.

"Surely there are several strategies that will achieve the same objectives. Why don't you present the alternatives, so we can choose one?"

Forget it. There are no alternatives to a powerful strategy developed from the bottom up. Management that believes so lives in a dream world.

The development of alternatives is a residue of top-down thinking. When you're sitting on top of a mountain, any hill looks climbable.

When you go down to the front, when you're down there in Reality Valley, you realize your options are severely limited. You are lucky if you can find one hill to take.

In a highly competitive society, you are going to be hard-pressed to come up with one tactic that will work. Prize it. Accept no substitutes.

Yet marketing people often think the opposite. They see success as the sum total of a lot of small efforts beautifully executed. They think they can pick and choose from a number of different strategies and still be successful as long as they do a terrific job of execution.

We believe in the single-bold-stroke approach to marketing. In any given situation we believe you can find only one move that will work.

Your job is to find it and sell it.

When the personal agenda gets in the way

One of the major pitfalls in selling a program to Corporate America is the conflict between the personal agenda and the product agenda.

Some managers make decisions on the basis of, first, their impact on the decision maker's career and, second, their impact on the competition or the enemy.

Field-Marshal Bernard Montgomery's launch of an ill-fated offensive through Holland in World War II has been characterized by many as an attempt for personal glory at the expense of good tactics.

General George S. Patton, on the other hand, often put his career in jeopardy in order to exploit his highly successful tank tactics.

Many senior executives let their personal agendas keep them from making bold moves. Why take any risks when a person already has a high salary and a relatively short time to retirement?

Many junior executives let their personal agendas dictate "safe" decisions so as not to disrupt their progress up the corporate ladder. They remember the old adage, "A large number of those on the leading edge fall off."

In some American companies nothing gets done unless it benefits the personal agenda of someone in top management. Ideas get rejected, not because they aren't fundamentally sound but because no one in management will personally benefit from them.

One benefit of the Japanese "management by consensus" system is that it tends to block the personal agenda factor. A Japanese company focuses on the success of the organization, not on the success of the individual.

No one would suggest that we emulate the Japanese by depersonalizing our companies. Would we want to trade Lee Iacocca for Shoichiro Irimajiri, Yukiyasu Toyo, or Masahiko Zaitsu, the head honchos of Honda, Toyota, and Nissan? But perhaps there is a middle ground.

The champion system

One way to defuse the personal agenda factor is to bring it out in the open. Companies like 3M use a "champion" system to publicly identify the person who will benefit from the success of a new product or venture.

Buried deep in 3M culture is the philosophy that nothing is going to be approved unless there is a manager who will "champion" the project.

The successful introduction of Post-it Note Pads illustrates how the concept works. Art Fry is the 3M scientist who championed the concept that took almost a dozen years to bring to market.

Although the champion system works, it's not necessarily the best way. In theory, the ideal environment would allow management to judge a concept on its merits, not on whom it will meritorize.

If a company is going to operate the ideal way, it will take teamwork, esprit de corps, and a self-sacrificing leader.

One immediately thinks of Patton and his Third Army and its dash across France. No army in history took as much territory and as many prisoners in as short a period of time.

Patton's reward? Eisenhower fired him.

When the organization chart gets in the way

This often happens in large multidivision companies. You might expect it to happen when you're working from the bottom up.

Oftentimes the organization chart gets in the way of developing the tactic into a strategy. Perhaps the tactic involves more than one product or more than one market. If the corporation is divided into product or marketing divisions, you have a problem, a real problem.

To get the program launched, you have to cut across boxes on the organization chart. Selling a program internally is like running an obstacle course. People who have to approve the program and work together to implement it have other axes to grind.

Fundamentally, managers don't want to share anything, especially the credit for a successful program. They would rather do their own thing, even if it's only a moderate success, than be part of a larger, exceptionally successful endeavor.

What can you do to fight the organization chart? We recommend bottom-up selling. You have to grit your teeth and work your way up the organization until you reach the one person who can authorize programs that cut across boxes. (Perhaps that person can also change the names in the boxes.)

Don't try to short-circuit the system by starting at the top. When you do, you open the door for internal guerrilla warfare. As the program works its way down the organization, the long knives will be out every step of the way. You can be certain that the tenants in those boxes will think of objections that never occurred to you.

By exposing and dealing with these objections on the way up, you'll greatly increase your chance of success after you get top management's endorsement.

Bottom-up selling has its own special problems, of course. The "tendency to tinker" is the major one. (The road to disaster is paved with improvements.)

When you're pushing a concept up the hill, people you meet along the way feel they have to make a contribution. Unless you're careful, you may not recognize your own idea when it gets to the boardroom.

When top management gets in the way

You may have a dynamite tactic and a brilliant strategy and still strike out in the boardroom.

Of all the managers in a company, the CEO and staff are usually the farthest from the front. They are the least likely to recognize the power of the tactic. "You want to call the car an Acura instead of a Honda?"

They don't think in terms of tactics. They think in terms of strategies. "Does this fit in with our corporate strategy, B.J.?"

You have to use subterfuge.

One of your best subterfuges is to sell the impact of your strategy on the "reputation" of the company. All too often "reputation" is ignored in marketing. This is a by-product of too much short-term thinking on the part of the company's middle managers with their own personal agendas.

When a company's reputation is weakened in a marketplace, the results are often reflected in the press. Look at the problems of General Motors and IBM. The mystique is gone. Customers are finding it easier to rationalize the search for alternatives.

By its very nature, a single bold stroke has the potential of enhancing your company's reputation. Use this fact to rally top management support for your program. After all, no manager can refuse to salute the corporate flag.

The name is the strategy

Quite often you can sell the strategy, but not the name.

Names are drenched in egos. If your recommendation calls for a name change, you have your problems cut out for you.

Keep in mind one principle: The name is the strategy. You can't sacrifice the name and still have an effective strategy.

With a name like LaSalle, the high-end Allanté automobile could have been a big success. With the Cadillac name, there was no hope.

With the Pillsbury name, there was no effective way for the company to move into the microwave popcorn business.

Names are important. The single most important marketing decision you can make is what to name the product. The name is at the core of the bottom-up process.

When you compromise on the name, you compromise the program. Better to accept an internal defeat on the name issue than to accept an inferior name and lose everything on the marketing battleground.

Stand your ground. Defend your name. Accept no substitutes.

When Nestlé introduced a freeze-dried instant coffee to compete with Maxim, Nestlé's American management wanted to call the product "Taster's Choice." Back at headquarters, the Swiss wanted to call the brand "Nescafé Gold."

The name battle raged back and forth over the Atlantic for almost two years. The locals won. Taster's Choice is a big success. Today it outsells Maxim ten to one.

"Tastes and smells like ground roast coffee," said the Taster's Choice ads. The name is a reflection of a powerful tactic of positioning the product against ground roast coffee.

Stand your grounds. Defend your name. The name is the strategy.

Global marketing strikes out

One reason the Swiss wanted the Nescafé Gold name was so the product could be marketed around the world with a single name.

One name, one strategy, one positioning. That's the goal of global marketing, the latest B-school fad.

In most of the countries of the world, Nescafé is the leading coffee brand. In some countries Nescafé has a market share in excess of 75 percent. Nescafé is a powerful worldwide brand. But not in the United States.

Top-down thinkers would probably agree with Swiss management. "Let's make Nescafé a more powerful global brand by putting the Nescafé Gold name on our freeze-dried product."

Bottom-up thinkers would probably agree ... but only in those markets where Nescafé already is the dominant brand. In the United States, where Nescafé is nowhere, bottom-up thinkers would demand a new name to go against the strong Maxwell House/Maxim competition.

The same principle applies to Datsun. Was it necessary to change the name to have one worldwide Nissan strategy? Yes, if you think top down.

No, if you think bottom up.

When every country in the world is similar, marketing will become a worldwide endeavor. When markets are similar, working the process from the bottom up will produce a single program which can be used everywhere.

Until that day happens, the most effective marketing program you can develop in one country won't necessarily work in another.

Working from the bottom up assures you of optimum programs in each country.

14

Getting the resources

New York City's schools chancellor, Dr. Richard R. Green, defined his philosophy in these words: "No task will be evaded merely because it is impossible."

Thoughts like that sound great in the boardroom, but when you go down to the front line, you are face to face with reality. It might be difficult to accept, but the impossible is impossible.

In marketing, nothing is possible without the resources to launch a program. By resources, we mean money.

With money you can buy the tools you need, be they a sales force, distribution, or advertising.

Without the dollars to finance these operations, all the skillful planning in the world won't buy you an ounce of market share.

It takes money to make money. In this over-communicated society, it takes a lot of money to make money.

While top management is often comfortable with approving a multimillion-dollar plant, a multimillion-dollar marketing program is a lot harder to get approved.

Any new idea (and marketing is basically a battle of ideas) requires up-front investing. Yet many companies would rather set advertising and marketing budgets as a percentage of sales. Which means that a new idea doesn't receive the necessary funding to give it the impact it needs to break through the media clutter.

Divide and lose

A number of years ago, the Seven-Up Company developed two exciting strategies to compete with the big cola companies. Both strategies exploited the tactical issue of caffeine in Coke and Pepsi.

One strategy was the introduction of Like, the world's first decaffeinated cola.

The other strategy was positioning 7-Up as the soft drink with "no caffeine." Since 7-Up was already established as the "Uncola," the alternative to Coke and Pepsi, the caffeine attack promised enormous benefits.

Which strategy should Seven-Up have used? Either might have worked, but unfortunately Seven-Up spread its resources and tried to do both at the same time.

When Coca-Cola and Pepsi-Cola struck back with decaffeinated colas, the picture darkened for Seven-Up.

With double the resources, it's likely that Seven-Up might have made its decaffeinated cola into a big winner. Instead, Like struggled along for a few years before it was killed. (In a sense, the introduction of decaffeinated Coke and Pepsi gave credibility to the Like brand.)

While the Seven-Up Company was more successful with the "no caffeine" program for its 7-Up soft drink, it's likely that greater resources would have turned a moderate success into a big winner.

Everywhere you look, you see companies spreading their resources when they should be concentrating them. In the same year that General Motors formed a joint venture with Toyota, it also announced the Saturn project. Both operations will produce similar products.

One wonders how much better off General Motors would be today if it had focused its resources on a single line of attack.

Even worse than not funding a new idea is underfunding. "Many assume that half efforts can be effective," says Clausewitz. "A small jump is easier than a large one, but no one wishing to cross a wide ditch would cross half of it first."

Let's say you've asked for a million dollars to launch a new program. Management responds: "What can you do for half a million?"

Your response ought to be, "We can wind up right in the middle of the ditch." Better not to launch a program at all than to launch one without the resources to do the job.

Your problem of getting the resources often takes two forms.

1. *The poor little company problem.* Small entrepreneurs are usually long on ideas but short on money to bring them to life. To succeed, a small company must solve the resource problem.

If you work for such a company, either you have to narrow your geographic focus and work on a regional basis or you have to go for help.

The regional approach is probably the best initial step since it gives you a chance to work things out and refine your program. Tom Monaghan started his Domino's pizza chain with one store. Once he had a tactical handle on what works and what doesn't work, he then went for help. In his case it was franchising the idea to others as he spread his concept across the country.

Another going-for-help approach could entail selling out to a large corporation with the resources and distribution to take your concept national.

The danger a small company faces is that of being knocked off by a large organization before it has a chance to gain momentum in the marketplace.

Selling does not mean selling out. In most cases, you can keep a piece of the action. It's better to be alive with 10 percent of the action than dead with 100 percent.

2. *The rich big company problem.* Big enterprises like General Motors are short on ideas but long on money. The problem is the money tends to get spread over a host of projects.

So when you've got an important idea, it's important that you get your hands on the money before it's all given away.

That's the main problem in big companies. They often squander their resources on many products and activities. This is one of the perils of decentralization.

In a typical decentralized company, every manager of an operation is given a budget to grind his or her ax.

Top managers like to spread the resources around to keep everyone relatively happy. Their main concern is keeping track of the totals.

In the game of bottom-up marketing, top management has to maximize opportunities by putting the bulk of the resources against the breakthrough idea or situation. Since this means robbing Peter to pay Paul, CEOs have to be prepared to make the tough money calls. Then to defend those decisions when they face those managers they rob from.

For this to happen, top management obviously will have to be a lot more involved in the tactical details of the battle in the marketplace.

Some companies do put most of their chips on their new horse. When IBM introduced the PC, it put 75 percent of its advertising budget behind the new product.

In its first year the PC accounted for less than 5 percent of the company's revenues. But it was more than money that prompted IBM's advertising decision. The PC represented the future.

Top management involvement

While bottom-up marketing can work for anyone at any level, it works best if understood and practiced by the top person.

When a bottom-up program is initiated by the CEO, the whole process of running the program up the ladder is unnecessary. A company's reaction time is greatly speeded up because the top people are in the best position to allocate corporate resources. They're just down the hall from the VP of finance.

When top management learns how to play the role of take-charge leaders, the entire marketing process will become much more effective.

This is the essence of competing with Japan, Inc. While the Japanese practice a variation of bottom-up marketing, they do it with lower-level people.

What America needs are more MacArthurs at the management level. Like most generals, Douglas MacArthur understood the essence of the bottom-up approach to waging war.

It also works in marketing.

15

Calling in the outsider

At some point you will need an "objectivity test."

It's difficult for an insider to have the kind of objectivity you need to resolve those final but critical details. Insiders are too close to the trees. They know too much.

The outsider has the advantage of ignorance. Not knowing all the internal details, the outsider is in a better position to see things the way a prospect would see them. Because of their objectivity, outsiders can be of critical help, especially in the selection of the tactic to use.

Selecting the tactic

You can see why top-down thinking is so destructive to the marketing process, especially when outsiders are involved. When you do the strategy first, you are in effect also dictating to the outsider the tactics that have to be used.

This is so because tactics are primarily concerned with external things. What's in the mind of the prospect? What trends are affecting the business? What positions are occupied by competitors?

The outsider is less useful in the development of strategy, which is primarily an internal affair. How do we reorganize the company to take maximum advantage of the tactical opportunity? How do we build, staff, and operate the strategic hammer that will drive the tactical nail?

What often happens in the top-down mode of operation is that none of the tactical choices are particularly effective. And the outsider reluctantly comes to this conclusion.

Does the outsider tell the client the strategy is wrong (quite possibly losing the account in the process)?

Or does the outsider recommend the best of the bad options? (After all, outsiders can always console themselves with the notion that "strategy comes first.")

Bottom-up marketing clarifies the role of the outsider. It puts the process in a logical order. It frees the outsider to explore the full range of tactical options without the artificial restrictions imposed by a strategy.

Both sides benefit.

Seeing the obvious

The outsider can help you see the "obvious tactical idea." Sometimes the toughest idea to sell is the obvious one. If an idea is obvious, everyone inside the company assumes that it has been tried before and it didn't work.

Yet the best ideas are obvious ideas. They're best because they quickly connect with customers and prospects. They can be implemented in the mind with a minimum investment.

Insiders often reject the obvious as being too simple. Since it's obvious to them, it must not be "new" to the marketplace.

That's not usually true. Prospects are seldom so mentally wrapped up in a company and its products that they are aware of the obvious idea.

When Uniroyal introduced the Nauga, the mythical creature responsible for Naugahyde, it was an instant success. The public was taken by this new and unique advertising concept.

Yet the Nauga was an old joke inside the company. It was too obvious an idea for the insider to see.

The outsider's role is not to let the obvious idea fall by the wayside without a thorough hearing.

Outsiders often bring a breath of fresh air to the conference room. Insiders can easily fall in love with their own products and services. They get caught up in corporate philosophy. They verbalize erroneous ideas so often that the ideas become real.

The outsider can blow away the corporate myths and bring reality into the discussion.

The perennial outsider:
the advertising agency

The one outsider that regularly strolls the halls of Corporate America is the representative from the advertising agency.

Who calls the shots in your relationship? Do you or does your advertising agency?

"We are a partnership," says the agency.

"We do," says the company, but they say it under their breath, or at least out of hearing of the agency.

Manufacturers of high-tech products such as computers and industrial equipment tend to call the advertising shots. They feel, with good reason, that their products are too technical for them to turn over the reins to their advertising agencies.

Manufacturers of low-tech products like beer and soda tend to let their agencies call more of the plays. (On the other hand, low-tech Procter & Gamble has a reputation for keeping tight control over all aspects of its advertising.)

Assuming the advertising agency plays the dominant role, the relationship is stable as long as things are going well.

When things go wrong, the relationship usually ends, sometimes as suddenly as a surgical strike in a war. (Agency people don't know what hit them.)

More and more, however, the company plays the dominant role. When things go right, there's plenty of credit to spread around. When things go right, many companies are even willing to let the agency claim to be in charge. (Some marriages work the same way.)

Bottom-up marketing can help resolve this ancient conflict. With the agency focused on the tactic and the client focused on the strategy, each side has a primary area of responsibility.

All you need to remember is that the tactic dictates the strategy. If you follow this order, the relationship should work smoothly.

When agencies lose their objectivity

Most companies value their ad agency partners for their objectivity. But some ad agencies have been on the job so long they behave more like insiders than outsiders.

What happens when your agency loses its objectivity? It can be awfully hard to tell, especially since you cannot be objective about yourself.

If you look carefully, there may be signs. When you express an idea, is your account executive too quick to say yes? Or too quick to say no? (Nobody is 100 percent right or 100 percent wrong.)

Does your agency belong to the Idea-of-the-Month Club? Are they only too happy to trot out a second idea if the first one gets shot down?

If you were facing a triple bypass operation, you would readily seek a second opinion. As a matter of fact, your physician might insist on it.

What's wrong with the same philosophy when millions of dollars worth of advertising are involved?

But beware. Before you go for that second opinion, be prepared for the objective advice you may receive. There is no way that someone's ox won't be gored. No one can come into a marketing situation and not bruise a few egos. The reason: Corporations are perpetual-motion machines.

No one will come into a company to deliver that second opinion and hear, "We're glad you're here. We haven't done anything in the past year while we've waited for your arrival." Of course, things are done and decisions are made. That's what people are paid to do.

The problems will come from those people who may not be doing the right thing. They will view the process as a threat and act accordingly.

Self-preservation is the strongest of all human instincts, so top management must be on guard to prevent the vested interests from prevailing over good thinking.

When countries lose their objectivity

Nowhere is outside objectivity more critical than in the positioning of a country in the minds of the traveling public.

People in charge of tourism are usually natives of the country being promoted. Unlike residents of a corporation, they have probably lived in their country most of their lives. They have vivid memories of how it used to be before all those land developers and highway builders got their hands on the beautiful countryside.

They know about the bad weather, the traffic jams, and the rest of a country's shortcomings. They take their country for granted. After all, how many Americans tour Europe before they visit the leading tourist destinations in the United States? A lot do.

How many Americans have seen the Grande Place in Brussels and haven't seen the Grand Canyon in Arizona?

The same lack of objectivity exists in other countries too. New Zealand is an interesting case in point.

As you may have noticed, a lot of Americans are starting to get interested in visiting Australia, thanks to Crocodile Dundee.

With more U.S. travelers making plans to go down under, it would seem to be an opportune time for New Zealand to get a piece of the action. After all, it's in the same neck of the woods, and it's no big deal to see both countries while you're at it.

(For those who haven't made the trip, you get to New Zealand by flying to Hawaii, hanging a left, and flying another nine hours or so. Australia is another four hours of flying time.)

So how does New Zealand cash in on the interest in Australia? Simple. Just supply the traveler with an idea about the country that will make it hard not to stop and visit.

Now for the not-so-simple part. What is that competitive mental angle that will steal some travel days from Australia?

In all the years that New Zealand advertised in the United States, it never landed on a simple compelling idea or "position." It kept changing its advertising every time a new head of tourism arrived. All that stuck in people's minds was the perception that New Zealand is a pretty place somewhere in the South Pacific with lots of sheep.

For those of you who have never toured New Zealand, it is a visually spectacular place. If Walt Disney ever builds a country, it will probably end up looking a lot like New Zealand.

Basically the country consists of two islands. The North Island is a lot like coastal California, only better. Big green hills, lots of water, and millions of sheep that keep the country perfectly manicured. The South Island is a lot like the Alps. Big, snow-covered mountains, fiords, lakes, no wide highways. Then throw in a volcano or so and some picturesque towns that could have been plucked from rural England. Truly unspoiled and magnificent.

With spectacular scenery to work with, it wasn't hard to develop a tactic to introduce New Zealand to America.

The television commercial posed a question and went on to answer it with pictures that matched the words.

"What is the most beautiful island in the world?"

"The candidate from the North has magnificent lakes, unspoiled beaches, and enchanting streams."

"The candidate from the South has majestic mountains, breathtaking fiords, and stunning settings."

"But you don't have to choose between these two islands. You can visit both in a single trip."

"Just ask your travel agent to send you to New Zealand, *the two most beautiful islands in the world.*"

The competitive mental angle of "the two most beautiful islands in the world" stunned New Zealanders who saw the prototype commercial. They didn't think of their country as islands. Nor did they see its beauty. They were too close and too modest.

16

Launching your program

When you're ready to launch your program, it's time to shift gears. Instead of a bottom-up approach, you should launch the program "top down."

In other words, when you're ready to execute the program, you should insist on a precise, carefully timed, top-down launch.

"Bottom up for planning, top down for execution" is the pattern we recommend. Yet it's fair to say most companies do just the opposite.

Top management plans strategy in an ivory tower. They issue strategic plans that spell out their objectives in broad general terms. Middle managers are expected to take care of the tactical details.

Meanwhile, at the front the strategic plans arrive in the gold or silver binders that are promptly put on the shelf unread. "We know what our customers need and want," say the sales force. "That stuff would just confuse them."

At the advertising agency, the creative folks pore over those same strategic plans to see if there's something ... anything ... they can use in the advertising.

Usually they do find something, but by the time it's modified, improved, and reconditioned, no one at the company recognizes it anymore. No matter, as long as it's creative.

The military approach

A military organization combines bottom-up planning with top-down execution.

Once a strategy is developed from the bottom up, a military organization insists on top-down execution, with little room for individual decisions by lower-level commanders.

Like a good football play, a good military attack has a seamless, flawless execution with each unit doing its predetermined job at exactly the right time and place.

That won't work in business, you might be thinking. But it does. It works every day at places like Hertz, Avis, and McDonald's.

The essence of a superb franchising organization is to write the book and then "do it by the book." When you have a powerful coherent marketing direction (strategy), you don't let the individual players change it.

The business approach

Business could benefit from similar military executions. Too often strategies that are planned at the top are then turned over to lower-level people, who are given great latitude for making tactical changes.

Sometimes this works. A flawed strategic plan can sometimes be saved by tactical changes made by lower-level people at the sales front.

But this is not an efficient way to plan and not an efficient way to operate. It causes great strains on the command fabric of a business organization.

You see this in many large companies today. Lower-level people, the field commanders of a business organization, will routinely operate in direct violation of the strategic directions issued by their "ivory tower" headquarters staff. The field commanders keep their jobs because they are tactically effective.

It's a waste. A company could be much more effective if its leaders went out into the field in the first place to build their corporate strategies from the bottom up.

There's an irony about top-down strategic planning. With all the talk about goals, objectives, plans, and mission statements, the truth is that most companies today are not strategically driven. They talk a good game, but in practice the opposite pattern occurs.

Everyone is out doing his or her own thing without following the consistent single bold stroke we have been discussing. In such companies, corporate strategy is like the artwork you hang on the walls of your home. It doesn't do anything, nobody pays attention to it, but you feel better knowing the pictures are there. Bare walls make people nervous, just as a company without a corporate strategy seems somehow incomplete.

Would it make any real difference if your company didn't have a corporate strategy? Be honest. Probably not.

Ask someone in your own organization what your company's strategic plans are. If you get a 2-inch-thick binder in answer to the question, you know your company doesn't really operate by the book.

The strategically driven company

The irony about bottom-up marketing is that the application of the concept will produce a company that is strategically driven, as opposed to a company that just talks the game.

When a company bases its strategy on a tactic that works, it becomes strategically driven. It has a powerful focus that can be expressed in a single concept, with simple words.

Domino's strategy is to dominate the pizza home delivery business with the "home delivery in 30 minutes or less, guaranteed" tactic. That's it. You don't need the 2-inch binder to explain the strategy. (Domino's does, however, use the 2-inch binder to explain the system in detail to its franchisees. It's a working tool that gets used, not an expression of corporate philosophy that sits on the shelf instead.)

The tactically driven company

A company that does its planning in the ivory tower and then issues its strategic plans to the troops in the usual poetic fashion of the corporate executive winds up just the opposite. It becomes a tactically driven company with no coherent marketing direction. It goes where the tide and the winds take it. Its future depends more on timing and luck than on planning and execution.

Companies can change. A drifting behemoth can become a driven corporate army with a strong sense of direction. But the change can't take place overnight.

The first step is to find a tactic that will work and then build it into a strategy.

Initially, the strategy won't encompass all of a company's products or divisions. It can't. Companies don't get out of control overnight. They drift out of control over a period of time. You can't transform an amorphous mass of products and services into a powerful marketing machine overnight.

Nor can you predict the future. Nor can you plan exactly how the process of concentration will develop over the years. To attempt to do so puts the planning process out of touch with reality.

The reality is the marketplace and the mind of the prospect. That's the place to start the focusing process. You have to start with a single program built around the strongest competitive mental angle you can find. Then see how this program affects other products and services.

You may have to modify the direction in the years ahead, just as an armored division moves around an obstacle in its path. But you can't know this in advance.

All is for naught if your first program doesn't get off the ground in a dramatic fashion.

Specifically, how should the program be launched?

The "big bang" approach

You never get a second chance to make a first impression. Important ideas should look important. (And if your idea is not important, go back to the front and find one that is.)

Also, a new idea desperately needs visibility, which is very difficult to achieve without a major media commitment.

You should always consider the "big bang" approach. Launch the program with as much media weight and as much impact as you can afford. This approach can help you overcome the kind of inertia that always exists.

People are not sitting around waiting for your new idea or product. You need up-front excitement to get the market's attention before you can sell them anything.

When Apple launched the Macintosh computer, it ran a 20-page "blockbuster" advertisement in the business press.

Companies have also used blockbuster television commercials on the NFL Super Bowl to launch new marketing programs.

In addition to striking hard, you want to strike quickly. No good idea stays lonely for very long.

In the old days you usually had time before competition arrived on the scene. No more. Sometimes you get copied as fast as they can fly to Taiwan and back. So it's important to get your program on the street as soon as possible. Even if you have to make some adjustments as you go.

It's not necessary to be perfect before launching your program. There's nothing wrong with the idea of perfection, but in striving for it you might sacrifice some of that big jump you hope to have on competition.

The "roll-out" approach

There's a flip side to the big bang. It's called the "roll-out" approach. This is the preferred launching ap-

proach of the smaller company when faced with much
larger competitors.

Instead of launching the program nationally with a
big bang, you launch in a single city or a state or a re-
gion. Then you roll the program out to other areas.
Presumably somewhere down the road it becomes a national program.

If you work for a small company, there are two reasons to prefer the roll-out to the big bang.

1. Small companies don't have the wherewithal to
   afford the big bang. Not only is it costly, but it
   also diverts funds from the building of the infra-
   structure you need to support a growing business. So it's better to roll things out on a geographic basis.

2. Small companies might not want to attract too
   much attention from their bigger competitors.
   By rolling things out slowly, there is less chance
   of your idea or product being noticed. And even
   if it is, your larger competitors might not think it
   poses much of a threat if it's perceived as a regional program rather than a national one.

Aggressiveness pays

Never sacrifice effectiveness, however, by toning down
your programs. Even if you work for a small company,
be aggressive.

Many companies hesitate to launch aggressive marketing programs because they don't want to offend
their competitors.

They seem to value camaraderie at the annual industry convention more than anything else, including the effectiveness of their marketing program.

That's a mistake. Offend them. Your enemies will respect you for it.

Respect moves a lot more merchandise than friendship. In this country, we buy 42 times as many automobiles from our former enemies, the Germans and the Japanese, as we buy from our former friends, the English and the French.

If you want someone to love you, be nice to them. If you want someone to respect you ... and to buy from you ... punch them in the nose.

17

Keeping things on track

After a successful launch, your next major problem is keeping things on track. This is the most difficult assignment of all.

Most managers do not understand the nature of strategy itself. They think of strategy as something that takes place over a specific period of time, as in long-term strategic planning.

Strategy unfolds over time but itself is timeless. Strategy is a coherent marketing direction.

That's why a five-year plan doesn't make sense. If you own the best tactical car and you've selected the best strategic road to drive it on, does it make sense to have goals at the end of Year 1, Year 2, etc.?

Do you slow down at the end of the year because you've exceeded your goal? Do you speed up if you've missed your target? If so, you'd better get another driver.

To win in marketing, as in car racing, you have to go all-out all the time.

Furthermore, the existence of a 5-year plan with healthy annual sales increases seriously underplays the importance of your competition. You can't predict the future because you can't predict what your competitors might do.

For example, during World War II, the Allied operation called Market-Garden ran into a panzer division on R&R. (To make Market-Garden work, Field-Marshal Bernard Montgomery's forces had to capture and hold five bridges in a row. Four out of five wasn't good enough, and the plan failed.) How could IBM's long-term mainframe plans foresee the rise of the mini-computer?

That's why the essence of keeping things on track is to pour it on while being alert to competitive moves.

Leading from the front

To keep the strategy on track, you must have lines of communication to the front. Most top managers are screened from what's really happening. The best way to avoid that is to be down at the front yourself.

Take the Battle of France. Where were the German panzer generals during the crucial first few days? Down at the front lines leading the advance troops.

Rommel, in particular, was a big believer in being where the action is. During the crossing of the Meuse, the biggest military barrier to the invasion of France, he was down at the river, helping his troops load the tanks on the barges.

The best leaders in a marketing war are the ones who lead from the front. In the automotive wars, for example, Lee Iacocca's style is much better than Roger Smith's.

Reinforcing success

Reinforce success. Abandon failure. This ancient military maxim is often violated by business today.

The essence of military success is to feed the gasoline and supplies to the tank commanders making the most progress. And shut off the supplies to the tank commanders who have gotten themselves bogged down.

Most companies do just the opposite. Let's say a company has five product lines. Three are winners; two are losers. Guess whom management spends most of its time and attention with? That's right, the losers.

Shoot the losers. Feed the resources to the winners. This is sound military strategy, and it is sound marketing strategy too.

One reason managers hesitate to eliminate the losers is that they believe it reflects on their reputations. So they continue to prop them up with TLC and do-re-mi.

And guess where the money to finance the losers comes from? That's right, the winners.

Managers often justify these decisions with predictions of a glowing future ... always 3 to 5 years away. The greater the losses, the more rosy the predictions become.

Yet the history of marketing shows the reverse is usually the case.

Early losses are usually followed by even greater losses as the loser tries to reinforce failure. RCA's attack on IBM's computer position, for example.

On the other hand, early success is usually followed by even bigger gains. The 914 was an instant sales success when Xerox launched it.

Companies that continue to pour resources into lost causes should pay heed to Federal Express. You can't live in the future.

You can only live in the present. Federal Express zapped Zapmail because it was a loser. Another three years of Zapmail losses and Federal Express itself could have been in trouble.

When you abandon failure, you're in a much better financial position to reinforce success when it does come.

Keeping centralized

Companies that experience rapid growth are usually centralized. It's only after a big success that they decide to decentralize. "We've gotten too big to keep track of all our divisions."

That's when the growth suddenly slows down.

A decentralized company is closer to the front, but it is usually not able to turn an effective tactic into a strategy.

The various divisions may know what's going on and have a number of tactical successes, but they are not organized to play the bottom-up marketing game. They can't turn a tactical success into a single corporate strategy.

Take ITT, which had become an unmanageable mess. Most of the businesses acquired by Harold Geneen are now being sold off, but the real problem is

ITT's core business, telecommunications. At this stage of the game, ITT should have been in the same league as IBM and AT&T. It's another case of resources being frittered away on side battles instead of being concentrated on the main event.

To add insult to injury, ITT recently threw in the towel on its telecommunications business, the jewel of the ITT crown. ITT Telecommunications is now owned by Compagnie Général d'Electricité, a state-owned French conglomerate.

There is no decentralization in war. An army never goes into battle with a decentralized organization. No field commander would allow divisions to operate independently. Rather the commander keeps each unit under tight control. Woe unto the divisional general who fails to start an attack on time or fails to halt the troops at the stopline.

Some traditionally decentralized companies are changing. At General Electric, for example, Jack Welch is tightening his grip on the corporation with significant results. So is John Reed at Citibank.

For the most part, these examples are exceptions. At a time when business needs big thinkers, most companies are moving in the opposite direction. Using decentralization as an excuse to keep themselves out of the battle, corporate chieftains are doing themselves—and their companies—a disservice.

Keeping focused

Decentralization is pushing the planning process down the ladder. One Fortune 500 company bragged that half its managers are involved in strategic planning. (Patton's Third Army had 105 generals and one strategic planner.)

The more people involved in the planning process, the less likely a company is to come up with a brilliant strategy. Companies need to push the planning process up the ladder, not down.

There is a paradox here. To find a tactic that will work, you have to be closer to the front. To turn that tactic into a strategy, it helps to be closer to the top of the organization.

On the surface it might seem that a decentralized company is closer to the front. But that's an illusion because there's no way to turn any tactics that might be found into a coherent marketing direction.

A decentralized company is like an octopus with a lot of tactical sensitivity in its tentacles and no brain to select one tentacle and turn it into a strategy. The flesh is willing but the spirit is weak.

It's the risk-taking spirit of top management that's the first to go in a decentralized company. Managers are not dummies. They know that if they can somehow get above the "firing line," they can coast to the top of their corporation, where a golden parachute waits to cushion the fall in case of a merger.

It's easy to tell whether you're above or below the firing line. You're below the firing line if you can be fired for not achieving market objectives. You're above the line when you can't be fired for not achieving market objectives.

When you're above the line, those objectives are no longer personal. Naturally, you take credit for the successes in your area and you have the luxury of being able to blame others for the failures. You've achieved tenure in the corporation. A nice position to be in, but one far removed from the business itself.

You've become another figurehead on the corporate ship of state.

Consolidating operations

As decentralization has pushed the firing line lower and lower, companies have wound up with a collection of fiefdoms, none of which is powerful enough to launch big programs on its own. So marketing at many companies today has degenerated into a collection of holding operations. You might call this the trench warfare of the business world.

The biggest opportunity in business today is to reverse the process of decentralization. Companies must start to consolidate units so that they're big and powerful enough to launch effective marketing campaigns.

Hewlett-Packard, for example, had three autonomous divisions making different (and incompatible) computers, all sold to the same market. Customers started to complain that the company didn't have a coherent strategy.

So HP stripped the divisions of their autonomy, placing them in one group under one manager. The first change: the products were made technologically compatible.

Decentralization cuts off corporate chiefs from the noise and confusion of the battleground. It tends to destroy their "battle sense," the rare quality that Alexander and Napoleon and other great miiitary leaders were endowed with.

Business today cries out for more field marshals, men and women willing to accept total responsibility for planning and directing a marketing campaign.

Too often, companies promote their best marketing people out of the firing line and up to meaningless staff positions.

One thinks of Burger King's CEO, J. Jeffrey Campbell, who was promoted to chairman of Pillsbury's restaurant group just when Burger King needed him the most.

Watching out for the wounded

When a new marketing strategy replaces or corrects an old idea or approach, it may also create a "wounded corporate animal." Watch out for this cat.

While the creators of the new idea may not realize it, their efforts may have embarrassed the defenders of the old idea or the status quo. Rather than lose gracefully, the person who has lost corporate status retreats to the tall grass and waits for an opportunity to attack and derail the fledgling idea before it picks up momentum.

The corporate infighter can be as deadly to your new program as your competition.

18

Sensing your success

You have selected a tactic that you know will work, your strategy is developed to reinforce the tactic over the long term, and you've launched the program with a big bang. How can you measure success?

First of all, you have to know what to look for. Don't expect instant financial success, but do expect some indication that your marketing message is getting talked about.

In other words, awareness is the first step in the purchase cycle.

Federal Express was not an instant financial success, but it did create a flurry of favorable articles in the press.

Sometimes even negative stories are an indication that the marketing message is starting to penetrate the mind of the prospect. When Honda launched the Acura, an enormous success, the first reports in the press were downbeat. "Honda Hits Early Snags in Effort to Enter the Luxury-Car Market," said a headline in *The Wall Street Journal.*

Like a trend, a long-term marketing success usually starts rather slowly. Then it picks up momentum.

If sales go up too quickly, you might have a "fad" on your hands. Look out, the drop can be severe. (Video games and hula hoops are two examples.)

Markets develop in waves. First are the early adapters. These consist of the "first on the block" crowd, the big mouths. They often read *Consumer Reports* and perceive themselves as experts. How well you're reaching these "influentials" is an important measure of your early success.

Another measure, though not easy to obtain, is that of "competitor discomfort." If your competition threatens to sue, you know your strategy has struck a responsive chord. (The McDonald's suit against Burger King over the "broiling, not frying" concept is typical.)

Trade journals can be as important as the consumer press. If your program is beginning to be picked up and written about, you have struck a responsive chord with those whose job it is to cover your industry.

If they are impressed, chances are you will also impress your prospects. Conversely, if you seem to be having a hard time generating interest or excitement with the press, you might have a problem on your hands.

No news is bad news.

It's not the size of the success that matters; it's the direction that counts. As long as things are moving in the right direction, you are creating a momentum that will be hard for your competition to stop.

Finally, don't divorce your advertising from sales as many companies do. "It's very hard to tie business performance directly to advertising," said the senior vice president for marketing at R. J. Reynolds. "A company or a brand could do very poorly despite having good advertising."

Marketing is a battle fought in the minds of the prospects. Good advertising does things to those minds.

If it doesn't, then the advertising is not good, no matter how many creative awards it might receive.

Madison Avenue motto: *It's easy to win an award if you're doing an ad for a client who doesn't have to sell anything.*

19

Pouring it on

"Too much of a good thing," said the late American original, Liberace, "is simply wonderful."

When you have a big winner, you want to go for broke. You want to pour it on. Your biggest protection from competitive inroads is a massive investment in resources. If you don't move fast enough, you let your competitors reap the rewards that your efforts have sown.

One problem is the annual budget. While a nice way to keep track of the money, it creates a system that has little flexibility in accommodating change.

Can you imagine a war based on an annual budget? It would go something like this: "Sorry, Colonel, you'll have to wait until January for reinforcements. That's when we get our new budget." The problem here is the missed opportunity.

Your program launch might result in a big mistake by your major competitor. The opportunity to exploit this opening could call for an important increase in money and effort. When next year's budget rolls around, it may be too late.

Shooting for share, not profits

As a market emerges, your No. 1 objective should be to establish a dominant market share. Too many companies want to take profits before they have consolidated their position.

What makes a company strong is not the product or the service. It's the position they own in the mind.

The strength of Hertz is in its leadership position, not the quality of its rent-a-car service. It's easier to stay on top than to get there.

Can you name a company that has overturned a leader? Crest did it in toothpaste, thanks to the American Dental Association's seal of approval. Budweiser did it in beer and Marlboro did it in cigarettes. But it rarely happens.

A survey of 25 leading brands from the year 1923 proves this point. Today, 20 of those brands are still in first place. Four are in second place and one is in fifth place.

Even changes in rank don't happen very often. If marketing were a horse race, it would be a deadly dull affair. In the 43 years since World War II, there has been only one change in position in the top three U.S. automobile companies.

In 1950 Ford Motor Company moved past Chrysler Corporation into second place. Since then the order has been General Motors, Ford, Chrysler all the way. Monotonous, isn't it?

The "stickiness" of a marketing race, the tendency for companies or brands to remain in the same position year after year, also underscores the importance of securing a good position in the first place. Improving your position might be difficult, but once you do, it becomes relatively easy to maintain that new position.

Breaking out of the pack

If marketing were a horse race, you could clearly see the importance of breaking out of the pack early.

When the Food and Drug Administration allowed the marketing of ibuprofen, American Home Products moved swiftly to get the upper hand.

Not only did it launch Advil with a massive advertising program; it also poured it on in the production side. It actually manufactured the product before it received FDA approval.

If that approval had not come through, millions of dollars' worth of Advil would have been bulldozed over. But the effort paid off. Today Advil is the dominant brand of ibuprofen.

When you do get on top, make sure the marketplace knows it. Too many companies take their leadership for granted and never exploit it. All this does is keep the door open for competition. If you get the chance, slam the door in their face. America loves the underdog, but they prefer to buy from the overdogs.

Never finance the company's losers with the earnings from the company's winner, which is a typical accounting trick in a multiproduct company. This dampens your ability to pour on the resources to your winners.

The single bold stroke you are developing needs money to maintain its momentum. Sitting on an early success will make you an easy target for competition.

Spend the money on today, and tomorrow will be well taken care of.

20

Cutting your losses

"In this world," wrote Benjamin Franklin, "nothing is certain but death and taxes."

In the world of marketing there is no such thing as certain success. If there were, the game would not be the challenge that it is.

If your marketing program doesn't move the needle, be prepared to cut your losses. Fighting to the last man and woman is unwise.

Corporate America thinks otherwise. Admitting failure is perceived as bad form. Trying harder is a badge of honor. And when things really get bad, knocking yourself out is the accepted corporate response.

For every Lee Iacocca who succeeds against the odds, there are a hundred nameless corporate commandos who die trying.

Corporate America is trained to charge rather than to retreat. "All we need is a better sales effort" is the battle cry for the troops in the trenches. It's up the hill again. And the losses continue to mount.

The truth is, marketing battles are almost never lost from lack of effort. Battles are lost for three reasons: (1) your strategy was wrong, (2) you attempted something beyond your resources, or (3) the totally unexpected occurred.

Perhaps the nature of your market has changed. Perhaps your competitor has devised a superior strategy.

The element of luck

Then there's luck. In war as in marketing, luck plays a pivotal role.

Both Donald Trump and John Connally went out and bought everything in sight. Today one is worth billions and the other is bankrupt.

What's the difference between Big Don and Big John? About 1600 miles and 3 billion dollars.

Trump was lucky enough to buy Manhattan at the right time, and Connally was unlucky enough to buy Texas at the wrong time.

Trying harder wouldn't have helped Mr. Connally. Things are tough in the Lone Star State. (In a single year 20 Texas savings and loans managed to lose more than $4 billion. If a bank can't make money, what can you expect of a private citizen?)

The graceful retreat

This should be a major course at the Harvard Business School.

Many executives approach marketing as if the present battle were their only battle. Marketing is a series of battles. The trick is to win more of them than your competitor does. Squandering your resources on a lost cause will only hurt your chances to win the next one.

If your present tactic appears to be blocked, the sooner you halt the operation, the sooner you can try a new approach. Also, the sooner you halt a losing tactical approach, the more resources you'll have when you try again.

Will running up a white flag too soon throw away a golden opportunity? There's always that danger. Marketing is a gamble.

History shows, however, that winning strategies usually show some signs of success from the very beginning. If all the early signs are negative, your chances are slim.

The most dangerous aspect of "long-term strategic planning" is the assumption that a truly significant long-range project will always create short-term losses. That assumption is why management often continues to throw in the dollars waiting for the pot of gold in the future.

USA Today has cost Gannett some $470 million in its first four years. Will the pot of gold arrive tomorrow for *USA Today?* Don't count on it.

The truth is, big long-term successes usually show at least some signs of success from Day One. Big financial disasters are usually disasters at the beginning too.

Wars offer the same lesson. Attacks that are successful are usually successful right away. The German panzers broke through the French lines at Sedan in the early days and were never stopped.

At Verdun in World War I, on the other hand, the early German attacks were failures, yet they continued the offensive for months with predictable results and enormous casualties.

Many companies adopt the same "human wave" approach to marketing. They throw more salespeople, more advertising, more of everything into a situation where there are few signs of success. They keep the situation alive when they would be better off if the marketing program were dead.

Regroup. Find a different tactic and change your strategy. Hopefully, the very reasons why the first program didn't work will give you the insights you need to make your next program a success.

You can learn more from losing than from winning. "Show me a millionaire," someone once said, "and I'll show you a person who has been broke at least three times."

21

Playing the game

Most marketing people have a dream. They see themselves at the head of the conference table issuing orders to a host of underlings.

In the background is a bank of computer terminals feeding those orders into a global message network.

Every day a visiting dignitary arrives with a bow and a message. "Congratulations. You have just won another marketing victory in Romania."

Every week a helicopter whisks you off to the local airport where the corporate jet is waiting to fly you on a red-carpet inspection tour somewhere in the world. Nothing too strenuous, you understand. The purpose is to show the corporate flag in places like Paris and Vienna.

Ah, the rewards of being the world's greatest marketing strategist. It's not just the money and the fame, of course. It's the thrill of the chase.

Also part of the dream is your background. Naturally you are a graduate of both Yale and the Harvard Business School, so you're not provincial in your thinking.

If that is your dream, this book won't do much for you.

Put your mind in the mud

What *Bottom-Up Marketing* has to offer you is just the opposite. To become a great strategist, you have to put your mind in the mud of the marketplace. You have to find your inspiration down at the front, in the ebb and flow of the great marketing battles taking place in the mind of the prospect.

It's no secret that most of the world's greatest military strategists started at the bottom. And they maintained their edge by never losing touch with the realities of war.

Carl von Clausewitz did not attend the best military schools, did not serve in the field under the best military minds, did not learn his profession from his superiors.

Clausewitz learned his military strategy the best way and the hardest way. By serving in the front line at some of the bloodiest and most famous battles of military history.

Jena. Borodino. Berezina. Waterloo. Clausewitz was there observing which tactics worked and which didn't work.

Every great strategic principle conceived in the mind of Clausewitz evolved out of the mud of the battleground, out of seeing men live and die, out of seeing battles won and lost.

Cameron Mackintosh, the producer of *Cats, Les Miserables,* and *The Phantom of the Opera,* the three most successful musicals of modern times, began his career as a stagehand at the age of 18. Later he was stage manager of a touring show. At 23 he produced his first show, which resulted in a total loss for his backers.

Mackintosh persisted, producing British touring versions of *Oklahoma!* and *My Fair Lady.*

"I learned a lot about the craft of the musical working on these classics," he said. "Today I'm a hands-on producer, involved in every aspect of a production."

If you want to think great strategic thoughts, there is no substitute for immersing yourself in the tactics, whether they be military battles, musical battles, or marketing battles.

Gates, Monaghan, and Smith

The tactic dictates the strategy, in business as well as war. The greatest strategic successes of the past few decades were conceived by people who were thoroughly tuned in to the tactical marketplace they came to dominate.

Consider William H. Gates III of Microsoft, the world's largest programming company. A Harvard dropout, Gates went from being the world's youngest computer programmer to being the world's youngest chairman of a Fortune 1000 company.

Can it be hard to conclude that Bill Gates is a great corporate strategist because he intimately knows the tactical problems of his field? It's hard to conclude otherwise.

Consider Thomas S. Monaghan of Domino's Pizza, the world's largest home-delivery pizza chain.

Monaghan was barely out of high school when he bought a pizza store in Ypsilanti with a $900 loan. Today Domino's has more than 4000 outlets which bring in almost $2 billion in revenues.

Monaghan has flipped more pizzas than almost any other human being. You might say his strategy evolved out of the dough of the marketplace.

Consider Frederick W. Smith of Federal Express, the world's largest air freight company.

While Monaghan was flipping pizzas, Smith was flying airplanes in Vietnam, thinking about an idea for a new air freight service.

Today Federal Express is a billion-dollar company which dominates the overnight delivery business with a market share in excess of 50 percent.

Smith, Monaghan, and Gates all were intimately involved with tactics, yet their companies developed brilliant strategies which propelled them to the top. The tactics dictated their strategies.

What about you?

What are your chances to make it big like Bill Gates, Tom Monaghan, and Fred Smith?

Small. Luck cuts both ways, up and down. To make it big, you need a good idea and you have to be in the right place at the right time.

But marketing is not just the thrill of victory or the agony of defeat. It's also a game. And playing the game well can be its own reward.

To play the game well, you have to start at the bottom. Perhaps not physically at the bottom as Tom Monaghan did, but certainly mentally at the bottom.

You have to put your mind on the tactics of the battle you want to win. You have to focus on your competitors and their strengths and weaknesses in the mind. You have to search out that one key tactic that will work in the mental battleground.

Then you have to be willing to focus all of your efforts to develop a coherent strategy to exploit that single tactic.

You have to be willing to make changes inside the organization in order to exploit the opportunities on the outside. You can't change the environment, so don't try. Change your organization instead.

You can't be all things to all people. You have to resist the temptation to spread your forces, to fight dozens of small battles which drain your resources and rob you of the ability to win the big one.

Furthermore, you have to be willing to change your strategy if it doesn't work out. No one can predict the future. Life is a gamble. Marketing is a gamble.

But if you do your thinking right, if you go down to the front and find a tactic that will work and build it into a strategy, your chances of success are very good.

Even if your marketing victory doesn't go into the history books, success is always something you can put into the bank.

Index

About the Authors

With their two previous books, *Positioning* and *Marketing Warfare*, and now with *Bottom-Up Marketing*, authors Al Ries and Jack Trout have firmly established themselves as leading-edge thinkers in the marketing and advertising world.

Their revolutionary ideas have taken shape over the past decade, owing largely to a rigorous schedule of speaking, writing, and consulting activities. They head a New York City marketing firm (Trout & Ries Inc.) which has developed marketing tactics and strategies for many of America's major corporations.